The Best
of Bad
Hemingway,
Volume Two

A Harvest/HBJ Original
Harcourt
Brace
Jovanovich

San Diego   New York   London

▼▼▼▼▼▼▼▼▼▼▼▼

The Best of Bad Hemingway, Volume Two

▼

MORE CHOICE ENTRIES FROM
THE HARRY'S BAR & AMERICAN GRILL
IMITATION HEMINGWAY COMPETITION

INTRODUCTION BY
DIGBY DIEHL

Library of Congress Cataloging-in-Publication Data
The Best of bad Hemingway : choice entries from the Harry's Bar &
American Grill imitation Hemingway competition/introduction by
George Plimpton.—1st ed.
p.   cm.
ISBN 0-15-611866-1
1. Parodies. 2. Hemingway, Ernest, 1899–1961—Parodies,
imitations, etc.
PN6149.P3B47   1989
818'.54'080351—dc19   88-26809

Printed in the United States of America

CONTENTS

CONTENTS

CONTENTS

▶ *vii* ◀

CONTENTS

CONTENTS

CONTENTS

*Illustrations by David Levine,
Gerry Gersten, Rick Geary, Tullio Pericoli,
and Richard Thompson appear on pages 2, 26,
60, 104, and 114, respectively.*

Introduction:
Confessions Of An
International Imitation Hemingway
Contest Judge

We're baaa-aaack! Bad Hemingway fans, rejoice! You hold in your hands yet a second volume of irreverent, audacious, and sometimes downright silly parodies of America's 1954 Nobel laureate. As if this were not a sufficient outrage, after a hiatus of three years (to allow the swollen livers of the judges to regenerate), the International Imitation Hemingway Competition itself has been revived to coincide with the celebration of the twentieth anniversary of Harry's Bar & American Grill in Century City. The Torrents of Spring 1992 will be filled with Papa parody.

I helped foment the resuscitation of the Imitation Hemingway Contest, and even in doing so had known fear. After eleven years of sitting in Harry's staring at *bellini*-soaked entries for the International Imitation Hemingway Competition, I worried that I might have read too much bad Hemingway—thousands of words of comic homage. If I keep this up, I said to myself, eventually I will have read more bad Hemingway than I have read real Hemingway. Would it corrupt me? Was I jaded? Bored? Blasé? I knew that I had acquired immunity to bullfight jokes and was becoming weary of double entendres about snow leopards and Key

West. Nevertheless, I felt a certain exhilaration about being reunited with my fellow judges—the same sort of excitement which a *torero* must feel when returning to the ring for the first time after having been gored while executing a *veronica*.

Why do we do this? It is true that there has developed a marvelous camaraderie among the judges. Like a rite of spring, all of us look forward to the annual renewal of old friendships in the guise of exchanging literary opinions and communing over wine and good food. For strictly extra-literary reasons, we revel in the chance to separate the "good bad Hemingway" from the "bad bad Hemingway," to use Ray Bradbury's description.

But more to the point, why do you do this? Why this insane fervor to parody a writer who died thirty years ago? During the first decade of the competition, Harry's received over 22,000 entries and, in fact, they continued to get entries in the three years when the contest lapsed. When the first volume of *The Best of Bad Hemingway* was published in 1989, bookstores were amazed at the brisk sales. Now public clamor for more has resulted in this second volume.

Always more than just a great writer, Ernest Hemingway lived a quintessentially romantic life. Even before he died, he had already become an American icon, a symbol of rugged individualism, masculinity, and bravery—and he died the same way that he lived. A hard-drinking sportsman, he fought the Fascists in both world wars. In short, he embodied a lot of what America likes best about itself.

With his bare-knuckled, undandified prose, he was as much a hero to the working man as he was to the *literati*. With simple declarative sentences, his tales appealed to the same broad audience as radio thrillers and, later, prime-time network television shows. The stories he wrote about safaris in Africa, bullfighting in Spain, deep-sea fishing in the Caribbean, and passionate affairs of the heart were the very stories he lived, and everyone knew it. He consumed his life in his writing and hung it out there in black and white.

Do people still read Hemingway, or is he too hairy-chested for this age of feminism, recycling, and lite beer? From the Imitation Hemingway entries, it was always evident that some contestants knew more about the myth than about the prose. Often the spoofers tried to find humor by overlaying the superficial hallmarks of his robust style on such flyweight topics as yuppies, aerobics, or Valley Girls— the result was not unlike Madonna voguing her way through "The Star Spangled Banner" without knowing the words. But it was equally evident that this contest had sent many aspiring parodists scampering off their bar stools and back to dusty copies of *The Sun Also Rises, A Farewell To Arms, Death In the Afternoon,* and *The Old Man and the Sea.* In this second volume, almost every one of Hemingway's famous novels and short stories are referenced with appropriate irreverence. A few I even recall having read with approval on Judgment Night.

Each year of the contest, the number of entries became more voluminous, and it soon became impossible for the judges to read every gem among the thousands submitted.

Consequently the sponsors enlisted a number of local university English professors to read through the entries, and pass on only twenty to the judges to pore over on Judgment Night. College insecurities lingering, we judges became distrustful of the academic screeners, and there was always the suspicion among the sages at the Judgment Table that some of the best stuff had been winnowed out before we got to it. Some of what survived was funny, but it was not Hemingway; some of it was Hemingway, but it was not funny, and we obscenitied on much of it.

Here, however, is a collection of good and truly funny Hemingway, which I hope will be the second of many such volumes to be published as the contest continues. As it resumes, the rules of the competition and the prize will remain the same (see details on page 127) with the only innovation—and certainly a welcome one—being that the contest will be cosponsored by the Los Angeles PEN Center and that Judgment Night will be a benefit for PEN, a writers' organization dedicated to freedom of expression around the world.

Hemingway himself did not approve of this type of lampoonery, good-natured or otherwise, damning it to a literary hell one step below graffiti in the men's room. He may have been above it, but the rest of us are not. The good and true reason why we participate in the Imitation Hemingway Contest, both judges and entrants alike, is respect and admiration—for both Hemingway's work and the uncompromising way he lived his life.

The proof will come, as it always does, on Judgment Night. Amidst the frivolity of the evening, there is always the traditional toast "... To Papa." It will be a moment of great solemnity, and we will remember, and it will be good to remember together.

—Digby Diehl

Across the Street and Street and Back into Harry's for Another Round

▼

MORE CHOICE ENTRIES FROM
THE COMPETITION

The Literati

*T*he marvelous thing is that it's painless," he said. "That's how you know when you have a winner."

"Is it really?"

"Absolutely. I'm awfully sorry about the odor though. That must bother you about the reading."

"Don't! Please don't."

"Look at them," he said. "Now is it sight or scent that brings them every year?"

The cot the man lay on was in Harry's Bar as he looked out onto the glare of Century City. There were half a dozen of the literati squatted obscenely, drinking absinthe, Strega, and cold white wine. The service was true and good in Harry's that day. They read and drank in this pleasant place in the middle of the Entertainment Center near the Shubert Theatre.

"They've been here since the day the contest started," he said. "Today's the first time any have sobered and lighted on the stools."

"I wish you wouldn't," she said.

"I'm only talking," he said. "It's much easier if I talk. But I don't want to bother you."

"You know it doesn't bother me. But please tell us what to do."

"You can read them yourselves, and that might help, though I doubt it. Or you can shoot me. You're a good shot now. I taught you, didn't I?"

"Please don't talk that way. Couldn't I read them to you?" she asked.

"Read what?"

"Anything in the bad Hemingway bag that we haven't read."

"I can't," he said. "Talking is the easiest. We quarrel, and that makes time pass."

"We don't quarrel. None of us ever wants to quarrel. Let's not quarrel anymore. No matter how bad the bad gets. Maybe we can read some real Hemingway. Maybe the Lord will come."

"I don't want to move," the man said. "No sense in moving now except to make it easier for you."

"That's cowardly."

"Can't you let a man die as comfortably as he can without calling him names? What's the sense of slanging me?"

"You're not going to die. You're just going to read."

"Don't be silly. The reading is killing me. Ask those bastards." He looked over to where the literati sat hunched down. One of them got down from his stool and waddled over to the man, the winning story in his fat hand.

"Harry! Bring the whiskey soda," the man said.

—*Gilbert Neil Amelio*

It Was the Start of the Fall Season

▶ ▶ ▶ ▶ ▶ *I*t was the start of the fall season as I looked out across the room they called the Green Room, past the worn avocado-colored shag rug to the olive-drab sofa that sat beneath a framed watercolor of an old mill on the other side. A man stood next to the picture. His face was puffy and pink, and he had on a red tie. They had told us not to wear red because it looked bad on tape, and the man had been glared at by a girl with a clipboard in her hands. The girl had whispered something to a man in a gray suit, and now the man in the red tie was rubbing sweat off his neck nervously.

Then the girl with the clipboard came back to our room and waved for us to follow her.

"Now?" asked the man in the red tie. I could tell he was afraid.

"Yes," the girl said. "Oh, yes. Yes. Yes. Yes." I could tell she was annoyed. We walked out to the stage. The man in the red tie stood on the left-hand side as you looked at it from the audience. I tried to remember if that was what they called stage left but could not. It was like starboard and port or dolphin and porpoise. You never could remember which was which when you needed to know it. That was just the way it was.

I stood on the right. Between us was a large wheel with numbers all around it. The numbers stood for points that we might later redeem for good and valuable prizes. The lights above us were very bright, and I wished I were back in Harry's Bar & American Grill. Harry's was clean and dark and smelled of good tobacco and single-malt scotch. I wished I were there gulping espresso because I had drunk an entire fiasco of Chianti the night before, and at that moment the lights on the set hurt my eyes. But that was all right. At least I had not been so careless as to wear a red tie.

Then suddenly the man in the gray suit strode out and stood between us, smiling, and a red light came on above the center camera, and I heard music like a thousand ill-tuned Spanish guitars stream from overhead. It was a great roar and confusion, and I wondered if my eyes showed fear like that in the eyes of the man in the red tie. I must have been afraid too, but I did not move. There was nothing else you could do but stand very still and answer the questions.

The man in the red tie took his turn first, but his words were not true, and each time he spoke a harsh bell sounded. His eyes were like a rabbit's just as it is caught by a fox, only the man did not make that high piercing scream they make just as the fox bites down through the soft fur and snaps the vertebrae at the base of the rabbit's skull.

"One more miss and you lose," the man in the gray suit said. He was still smiling, but his eyes were gray like his suit and hard, and the man in the red tie did not smile in return.

It was tragic, but I did not say anything because with a man like that it was no good to say anything. He was going to fail. He would not bring home any valuable prizes, and his wife would probably yell at him, and perhaps later in a darkened room he would begin to drink too much of the slow hemlock that is cheap blended scotch. The harder he struggled, the more he became entangled in his own confusion. He was like a porpoise caught in a gill net. Or was it a dolphin? Whatever. It was still no good.

The man in the red tie spun the wheel again. He rubbed sweat off his throat then answered the question. The man in the gray suit clapped and said, "Good answer, good answer," but then the bell sounded.

"Is that for—?"

"Don't ask," the man in the gray suit said.

Then they led the man in the red tie off the stage, and it was my turn next, my turn to face the Wheel and the Man in the Gray Suit, to try to win the stereo system or the bedroom set but perhaps just hear the bell and be ushered out. That was what you did. You tried. You did not know what it was about. They pushed you into the lights and told you the rules, and after three wrong answers they led you away. Maybe you would get a six-month supply of Rice-a-Roni and a case of nail-polish remover, but you wouldn't get the car. You could count on that. Say anything that came to your head, but you would never get the car.

—*Tom J. Astle*

AL'S WELFARE TO FARMS

▶ ▶ ▶ ▶ ▶ *I*t was morning and had been morning since late last night.

The man stood now on the mound in the middle of the cow pen silhouetted against the morning sun, wearing his mail-order cap which held a can of beer that the sun was beginning to warm, on either side.

The woman, rich and shallow, whose current amusement the man was, moved away from him now toward the gate with a graceful agility which indicated that she was socially superior to him and that she could beat him at Go Fish and also that she was wearing new Reeboks.

"You know what has to be done," he had said.

"Yes, my love," she had said. She was radiant. She was happy. Her eyes were blue. The sun was out, and the day was bright.

She stood at the gate now, Reeboks soiled in spite of her wealth, and as a dark van drove up the road, she looked with raw desire at the man on the dung hill siphoning beer from his cap through a long straw. Now he would prove himself, she thought.

Two men in Italian shoes, tailored suits, and dark glasses got out of the van that said Al's Welfare Wagon, Interest-free Loans to Farms on the side. One man cracked his knuckles as he looked around.

The man in the cow pen, sure now that he was a fine farmer and had to be a farmer and could be nothing else, waved his bandanna, and the woman with strong brown hands opened the gate and yelled and waved her arms at the cows who began to stampede with good, smooth skill since one of the heifers had learned the technique from a cousin who had run with greatness in Pamplona.

Each cow had painted on her side in white paint with fine strong strokes a message: Al Is No Pal, How Dare Welfare, and Eat at Harry's on a particularly renegade cow who refused to listen to anyone but Julio Iglesias sing "Louie, Louie."

Dust rose and filled the air. The two men turned and ran before the cows through the narrow callejón between the barn and the pigpen. One cow whose name was Bessie but who preferred to be called Babs tossed one of the men several yards with her horns, tearing his suit and drooling on his shoes. The man landed hard on the dirty ground. His friend helped him up, and the two ran and limped to their van and left quickly.

The cows returned to their pen triumphant, full of the elation that comes after a good stampede. The woman walked back to the mound in the middle of the cow pen and stood studying the face of the man whose victory was real and not idealistic, and she knew that he was a fine farmer and nothing else, and she would not beat him at Go Fish this day.

—*Gayle Briscoe*

FLOTSAM & JETSAM, MS., P. 37

Then the door swung open.

"These pants are welded steel," announced the stranger striding stiffly into Harry's Bar & American Grill.

"It was the best of times, and it was the worst of times," said Concha Ortega y Ruiz de Montoya, the whore who accompanied him. She was honest, and the men respected her. Even Harry the bartender. Harry made the best daiquiri in Florence. He squeezed the limes behind his knees. On the floor. He did it by himself, and it was hard. Not as hard as the Caesar salad but it was hard.

"What will you have?" asked Harry.

"Two bottles of Fundador, six bottles of Château d'Yquem chilled to the point that the moisture forms so heavy and wet on the bottle that you can't read the label just like in Ronda, a couple of your lesser reds, and a small Coke. The lady will have a stinger," said the stranger.

Harry looked at him. He did not look like a bullfighter. But it wasn't like it used to be. They didn't. He would have known if it was Belmonte. It wasn't. Joselito was dead and gored before his legs went, and it was hard.

"To go," asked Harry, "or do you want to drink it here?"

He knew the answer but asked anyway. He was a kind man in spite of the Great War and all it had done to him, and there would not be a time to forget. It showed, and he knew it.

"Here," said the stranger, reaching for the first bottle of Château d'Yquem with the moisture running down the sides, like the bulls in the streets of Pamplona, obliterating the label and making it hard. Just like in Ronda.

"Give me another estinger," said Concha Ortega y Ruiz de Montoya, glancing toward the door. She was a good whore, and the men respected her. She worked the side streets and didn't cause trouble, but it was hard.

"Sure," said Harry.

It was dark in Harry's Bar & American Grill. The stranger leaned over the zinc counter and looked Harry in the eye. "Do you fish?" asked the stranger. Harry shook his head. There had been a time before the Great War when he had threaded more black grasshoppers by the thorax than any other man alive but not anymore. It was too hard.

"Well, we can't all, and some of us don't," said the stranger, reaching stiffly

—*Sandra Borgrink*

ACROSS THE RIVER AND
INTO FORT LEE OR,
BETH IN THE AFTERNOON

▶ ▶ ▶ ▶ ▶ *A*t four o'clock I was in Murray's Sturgeon Shop waiting for Beth. She was not there, so I bought some fish. They were not very fresh fish, but I hoped that their costing six dollars a pound would help them. Beth did not turn up, so I went over to the Argos and had a coffee with Nikos the counterman. Beth had not been there either, and so I walked along the sidewalk to Zabar's. The sidewalk looked dirty, but then it always did. The sidewalks would always be dirty on the West Side. If one started out clean and shiny, it would take longer to get dirty, but the dirt would always win out. That is the thing about sidewalks.

After a while I walked into Zabar's. There are two levels in Zabar's. One is upstairs and has kitchen accessories. You have to have plenty of money to buy them. There are copper pans hanging from the ceiling, and below them you can see the tops of people's heads moving back and forth. But you could not see Beth. Then I went downstairs and looked at the cheese. There was a woman leaning over the cheddars. It was Beth. She was wearing a Yankees cap, and I saw a clerk looking at her. His face had that yellowish color that clerks get in the afternoon, but he seemed not to notice.

"Well, here you are," I said. "Looking at the cheeses."

Beth turned and kissed me coolly on the forehead. "Hello, darling," she said. "Let's buy some Edam, shall we?"

Suddenly I felt tired and unpleasant. To hell with Edam anyway, I thought. It looked rotten, and looking at it I thought the whole city looked rotten. Enjoying life was learning to ignore how rotten most cheese looked. It seemed like a silly philosophy. In five minutes, I thought, it will seem finer than any I'd ever had.

"Oh, Beth. Let's change our lives and move to New Jersey."

"Darling. Please, let's not talk about it. Talk is bilge."

"Yes."

"*Would* you buy a lady some tabbouleh?"

I bought a quart of tabbouleh and a rye bread. We took a taxi uptown. I settled back against the cool seat. Beth leaned toward the window. Past her I could see the sun going down over Fort Lee.

"Oh, darling," she said. "I've been so hungry. We'll go have a good dinner, won't we?"

I smiled and said yes and looked out the window. It did not matter where you moved in the world. You would always be looking at the good life across the river from a taxi that smelled of fish. Another silly philosophy. Damn philosophy, anyway. Damn Beth Axelrod. Damn the Yankees.

"Let's stop off and have a drink at Harry's Bar," I said.

"Splendid. But it's in Florence, you know." She lifted her hand to my cheek. "Poor darling. You're just hungry."

"Don't be sentimental."

We kissed, and she handed me an egg. It looked like a fine egg. I peeled it and took a bite, but it was no good. It is awfully easy to eat hard-boiled eggs in the daytime, but at night it is another thing.

—*Robert Cohen*

THE BLACK DOG CAME TO THEM

▶ ▶ ▶ ▶ ▶ *T*he black dog came to them at the base of the mountain. It was a great beast with massive jaws and teeth as thick as two fingers. He looked at the girl, but there was no fear in her.

"Was it good for you?"

"As never before."

Her dark eyes flashed with pride as they searched his and found only truth.

He moved slowly once more across the broad, white flank of the mountain, drawing her with him into its alpine shadow. This is truly a woman, he thought. Not once on the long trek had she complained. Yet had he not sensed her spirit that wet afternoon in Harry's Bar where he saw her drink a fine, clean anzo with her steak tartare?

"I felt as if I were falling from the mountain. Will it be as good again?" Her breath was hot against his chest.

He turned and saw the black dog lope away in pursuit of a frantic mouse. A deep sadness came upon him, and he shook his head.

"We are fools to tempt the mountain twice."

"I am your woman. I will go where you will. Let us obscenity on this Matterhorn!"

"You are as wise as you are strong." He held her close. They looked away from the mountain and followed Goofy and Mickey to the Teacups.

—*Michael A. Cowell*

THE BIG TYPEWRITER

▶ ▶ ▶ ▶ ▶ *T*here was paper on her desk in the little adobe room. There was writing on the paper. It worried him.

She worried him, too. Ah, she was a streeply woman. But she was a woman of childbearing age. She wanted her own typewriter. Girls did not have typewriters. Typewriters were man things. He knew this.

"What about the other ones?" he asked.

"The others?"

"Yes."

"Their typewriters were too small." She sighed without sadness. She did not regret using their typewriters, but now she did not care about them anymore.

He did not want to talk about the keys and platens of the others. He was sorry that he did not show her his machine after dinner last night.

"You were nice to the waiter at Harry's," he said. "It is one of the things to look for. It says so in *Nice Guys Sleep Alone.*"

"Did Hemingway write that?" she asked, but she knew

it did not matter. A smile played at her lips. He wanted to play at them, too.

"I like you," she said. "You are not bald."

He began to worry about the size of his typewriter.

"You do not care that I am not gunly?"

She thought about the other ones. The ones with big Winchesters and small Olivettis. The ones with no hair.

"No. I do not care," she said. She wanted him to worry, but only a little.

"Trust me," she said. "I was a touch-typist during the war."

He knew then that she knew how to handle a typewriter. He was happy that he still had one.

—*Julie Robertson*

As I Stepped Out of the Door
of the Century Plaza Hotel

▶ ▶ ▶ ▶ ▶ *A*s I stepped out of the door of the Century Plaza Hotel I came out into the early morning sunlight of Los Angeles, which is like no other sunlight in the world. Well, I came across into the shade of the passageway beneath the Avenue of the Stars to get coffee, and there was only one producer in sight, and he was sitting at an outdoor table attached to the marble floor waiting for a pigeon. But when I got inside the café and sat down, there were the three of them waiting for me.

I sat down, and the associate producer came over. "Look who's here," he said.

I looked at his matching belt and shoes and bag that were the color of a bull's blood that is drying but not completely dry. He ran his fingers over the belt. "Cootchie," he said.

I had not liked him at the party, and I liked him less now. Keep your temper, boy, I told myself. Don't let him spoil it.

The other two had come over, and they stood there arguing. "It's in *turnaround*," the co-executive producer who didn't button his shirt said. "Hey," the associate producer said, "let's forget about that other *piece of shit*, okay?"

It was beginning to seem natural, no longer to be itali-cized, just as the chest jewelry came to seem the proper and natural adornment and there was nothing odd or unseemly in the sniffing of powder before lunch, the women who held hands in public, or in a man carrying a purse.

"I'm sorry," I said, lying.

Now they surrounded me, and three colognes mingled. It was like copper pennies beneath my tongue. I remem-bered that when they find out definitely and for good that they have no talent, they become producers.

"Hey," the associate producer said, "this is the dude who wrote, 'I felt the earth move.'"

"Great song," the one who didn't button his shirt said.

"Just the line," I said, "not the song."

"Afterward, when it goes into syndication, it would mean a good deal to you." They were experienced producers, knew contracts thoroughly and invented clauses that were brought to the highest point of complication, ambiguous interpretation, and general difficulty and danger. The whole end of the action was the final contract, the actual entrap-ment of the one who can do things by the producers and their agents, what the Californians call the deal, and every move in the action was to prepare the talent for that mo-ment. I got hold of one of their thumbs and pulled it. "Let's go in Harry's for some Irish," I said. "I'll write a piece some time and put you guys in it."

—*Bruce Bebb*

THE OLD MAN AND THE SEA II:
THE SEQUEL

▶ ▶ ▶ ▶ ▶ *H*e was an old man who surfed alone on a longboard at Malibu, and he had gone years now without riding a wave. The old man was thin, and his Jams hung low on his hips. He had crow's-feet at the corners of his eyes from squinting while looking toward sea, and his skin was a deep brown.

Except for his hair, which was the same color as the sand, everything about him was old.

"Dude," the old man said to a young local as they stood on the sand watching the surfers at first point. "Did you see me hanging ten yesterday?"

The boy knew that the old man was senile, and he liked him.

"Yeah, you were shredding," the boy said.

"How's the swell today?" asked the old man.

"Two to three but it's closing out. The shape should be tubular at glass-off."

"Bitchin'," the old man said.

"Yeah," the boy said. "Want to spark a dube?"

"Why not? Between surfers."

They sat on towels on the beach between the pier and

the lifeguard station, and many of the bikini-clad girls, volleyball players, and Valleys gawked at the old man, and he did not notice. He was stoned.

The boy put on his wet suit and bootees and took his board from the trash can on which it leaned. They went down to the ocean, carrying their boards, and walked over the rocky tide pools toward the deep water.

The water was cold, and the old man said, "The water is cold. Surfing was rad, and now I am hungry. Aloha."

Although inflicted with Alzheimer's, the old man still remembered what was important. He had excellent taste, and evening found him at Harry's Bar speaking to a young and beautiful girl.

"Babe," he said, "I am a surfer."

The girl did not understand, and she asked her stock question: "Do you have any diseases?"

"No, but I have a ten-foot thruster."

"Oh," she said. "That sounds dangerous."

"You know a surfboard can be destroyed but not deflated."

—*Lee Silverman*

THE LAWYER AND THE CLARINETIST
OR, THE THREE-DAY BLOW

▶ ▶ ▶ ▶ ▶ Sidney Roberts and I stood at the bar in Harry's Bar & American Grill. Outside the sun was hot, but inside it was cool and the waiters were young and pleasant and the bar was polished. Sidney Roberts loved to get drunk at Harry's, but he did not want to get drunk now.

"You need a drink," I said. "What do you want?"

"Nada."

I ordered two nadas, and we drank them and ordered two more. I looked at poor Sidney Roberts. He was a lawyer, and his girl was a concert clarinetist. He loved her very much and would do anything for her. Sidney Roberts had given her a reed he had made by hand for her clarinet. She did not want it. She did not want Sidney Roberts anymore either.

"She said it was too small and thin."

"Show it to me."

"No."

"Come on."

"All right."

He opened his pocket and took out the reed.

"It's adequate," I said. I ordered two more nadas.

"She said it would break."

"But afterward, it is always strongest in the broken places."

"Her friend, the oboist, said it would not last an hour."

"Oboe *loco mas*."

It began to rain. Now Sidney Roberts wanted to get drunk. That was what you did. When you did not have a woman, you had a drink. I drink all the time, but only in the good places like Harry's. Every day it is nada y nada, nada y nada.

So I stood there and drank another nada and looked at Sidney Roberts and his reed. I wanted to say something to the lawyer the girl had sent away, but it was like talking to a statute. Afterward, we went out of the bar and shadowboxed in the rain.

—*Gary D. Ford*

Down in Michigan
or, For Whom the Smells Toll

▶ ▶ ▶ ▶ ▶ *J*ack Thomas hung his net and leather rucksack on a broken branch in the stand of pines where he had made camp earlier and knelt down on the floor of pine needles to sweep out a small circle for the fire in the damp-smelling sand. He got up and picked up the kindling he had split that morning with the ax and made a small tepee and put a handful of pine needles and twigs in the center. It was twilight, and he could hear the wind through the pine trees. It had been a fine day. It was a good camp.

Jack reached through the mosquito netting of the tent and felt inside his mess kit for the matches.

The matchbox was small and white and dry with the words *Harry's Bar & American Grill* on it in red ink. It was Nice. He turned the matchbox over, and there was the address. It wasn't Nice. It was Florence. But it had been nice. Not Nice. How could he forget? Because you had to forget. Because if you remembered one thing you remembered every thing. And if you remembered every thing nothing was any good. But now it was too late.

Harry's was the last place he had seen her. It was a clean, well-enough lighted place. The waiters were good, and the wine was very fine, and they used to sit at a table by the street with people walking by and the smell of bread and garlic and minestrone coming from the back.

That last time they had been quiet for a very long time.

"Before you leave, I need to ask you something," he said.

"Do you want to?" She did something.

"Would I ask you if I didn't want to?"

"Ask me."

"What is that smell?"

"It's that bull's ear in my purse."

"I knew it wasn't the food. You should have left it in the dresser drawer of your hotel room in Pamplona."

"I know. I do feel such a bitch." She turned her head.

"I wish you wouldn't."

"I can't help it. I do feel such a bitch."

She was crying. He could feel her crying.

"Say something nice."

"The fettuccine florentino is very nice here."

"Can't you do any better than that?"

He did not say anything.

Jack Thomas struck a match. It flared up, and he stuck it into the center of the tepee and smelled the sulfur and heard the crackle of the pine needles catching the split kindling. He had to split more pieces of wood in order to make the fire good enough to cook on.

That was it. Don't think about anything. Split the wood and cook dinner. It had been a fine day. Don't spoil it now. There was the camp and the fire and today's catch, and it was good. He put the matchbox into the fire, and it caught and flared up. That's better. Don't think about anything but the camp and the smell of pine needles and the sound of the fire crackling and the wildness of the woods and today's catch.

Jack got up and went over to the tree where he had hung his net and rucksack to look at the day's catch.

He pulled the jar out of the smooth leather pack. It had stopped moving. The chloroform had taken effect and it was still, its black antennae quiet and its brown and gold speckled wings beautiful and not moving in the firelight. That was better. Tonight there was the fire and the pine needles, and tomorrow there would be more hunting and more country and another fire.

He would have to go back into town to get some matches. But that was tomorrow, and the fire needed more wood now.

—*Leif A. Gruenberg*

ABOUT NOTHING IN GENERAL

▶ ▶ ▶ ▶ ▶ *W*hat possessed you to do that?"

"Do what?"

"What you just did."

"I don't know."

"Well, don't do it."

"I was damn bored."

Jack was tight as hell, and when he was tight, he got to rambling on about things like stuffed dogs and about past love affairs and a girl named Sandy who rode imaginary bulls while shooting ducks in a stream. He liked to talk about gambling and drinking and what a fine chap he was and how much money he had and about nothing in general.

"Let's go to Harry's Bar."

"You're tight enough."

"I am not tight, I am just bored."

"All right, but don't be an ass!"

"I am never an ass!"

"All right, what's at Harry's Bar?"

"I just want to tell the lovable beast, the old gal, what a fine job she did in the shooting."
"You're tight."
"I know."

We walked across the street and into the high rises. Jack kept mumbling about losers taking everything and about girls in the dream screaming, *"Olé, Olé!"*

—*Susan Countryman*

THE GARDEN OF CRETINS

▶ ▶ ▶ ▶ ▶ *I*n the spring the miniature golf course was always there, and they went down to it every day. On the way they passed the 7-Eleven, and the young man bought them each a Mr. Pibb and Cheetos, and they sat on the curb drinking the carbonated beverage and eating the crunchy but substanceless snack. The Cheetos turned the young man's fingers yellow, and he told himself to remember this. If you don't remember one damn thing in your life, remember your fingers yellow from the Cheetos and the smell of exhaust in the parking lot and the splendid girl beside you.

"Will you kiss me now, please?" the girl asked. "And then we'll have some more of the Mr. Pibb, and afterward I'll grow a mustache. You won't think me odd, will you, darling? You'd like me to grow a mustache."

"Yes, but don't talk about it."

Then they went to the miniature golf course, and when he got to the last hole, there was the tension inside him, because he knew if he made a hole in one here, he would win a free game. As he was lining up the shot he could feel it start to go bad. What would she look like with a mustache anyway? For Christ's sake, he told himself, get ahold of yourself. Would you want the *types* at Harry's Bar to see you now? Think about your father. Do you want to end up like that? No, I didn't think you did. Then just tap the ball. Not hard but with the firmness and the softness.

He hit the ball and watched it roll. Forget about it now, he thought. There's nothing you can do about any of it. But he lay down anyway on his stomach to see better as he watched the ball move toward the cup. He could feel his heart beating on the green felt surface of the fairway.

—*Stephen Harrigan*

NICK WAS HUNGRY TO SIT

▶ ▶ ▶ ▶ ▶ *N*ick was hungry to sit. But first came the moving of the chair.

He took hold of the horns of the straight-backed chair. It was as smooth as wood. It did not burn his hands. It was a very fine experience.

Nick liked to pull out chairs from under tables. He liked the sound of the legs scraping the floor. He liked to look at the seat of a chair and to think about sitting there. That must be why chairs were built the way they were, Nick thought.

The best place to pull out chairs was Harry's. There, no one minded if you were serious about it. There, no one minded if you pulled out every chair in the place, as long as no one fell over.

Harry was a serious chair puller. He had played poker. He had pulled many squat chairs from under tables with eight sides. He had seen much green felt. It was a triumph.

That was a long time ago.

Two old men in tuxedos walked by Nick. They were smoking cigars. They made the smoke smooth and deep around them. They looked at Nick like he was nuts.

Nick lit a cigarette. He still held the chair with both hands. He laughed. That was a trick he learned in Italy during the war, from Maria.

Nick was very hungry to sit. He moved to the front of the chair and sat down. He felt rest coming. He sat there with a satisfactory feeling and looked at all the other chairs.

—*Marion Hodge*

HILLS LIKE GREEN GRASSHOPPERS

▶ ▶ ▶ ▶ ▶ *T*hey sat, at a table, in the shade of the railroad station between Barcelona and Madrid. A beaded curtain, with the painted *toro de oro*, separated the bar, inside the station, from the flies and the American couple who sat looking across the valley at the distant hills. The hills were green and jumped from time to time in the reflected heat.

"You know I love you—if only you didn't walk that way," she said. "But you always laugh when I do," he said. "I only laugh because you are so funny, and others laugh as well," she said. He shrugged and looked off at the distant moving hills. "It's pretty hot," she said. "Let's order something cool." "How about some cool green grasshoppers?" he asked. "Grasshoppers! You must think we're at Harry's place in Madrid," she replied. "Out here we are lucky to get green beer that is cold." He thought of the green hills that moved with dignity. *"Dos cervezas frías,"* she called through the beaded curtain.

The woman, from the bar, placed the glasses of beer on the two felt pads. "You could go to posture-training school," the girl continued. "It is really nothing, only a little time." He stiffened as she looked off at the hopping green mounds in the distant haze. "It is only a little thing, and then you would be perfect, and our life would be perfect," she said. "Will you please, please, please, please, please, please stop talking?" he asked. The felt pads under the half-empty glasses were damp in the heated shade.

The woman from the bar called through the curtains, *"La hora está, señores. El talgo viene en cinco minutos."* "What is she saying?" he asked. "She says the train is coming *muy pronto,*" she replied. Together they got up, and as he bounced without dignity through the beaded curtain, she carried the heavy bags, with the labels of many hotels, to the other side where the tracks looked toward Madrid.

The woman from the bar looked out at the empty tracks and wondered about the *gran ciudad de* Madrid. Where would the *señora* and the hopping *americano* go in such a city? Maybe to the place called Harry's Bar & American Grill, which is known to be clean and well-lighted and *muy simpático para americanos.* After all, in such a place they will serve the elegant drinks "hoppers *de verde,*" which the *señor* foolishly wished to order. Later the woman removed the two glasses and the stained felt pads and wiped clean the table of the American couple. Looking across the valley and into the hills she saw *gran hoppers de verde* rising and falling in the heated day. "It must be the sun," she said, "it also rises—*en nuestro tiempo.*"

—*Charles E. MacMahon*

THE WAY IT BEGAN

▶ ▶ ▶ ▶ ▶ *I*t was winter in Westwood and the restaurants were there, but you did not go to them anymore. You would walk through the streets and the hunger would be crisp and clear in the stomach, and you would pass a window and look at the women sitting in the booths with small desserts and glasses of champagne, and the smell of food would be coming out the doorway. After a while the waiter would come out and wipe your fingerprints from the window. He would throw the washcloth at you, and the hunger made you see sharp and clear, and you would laugh. You would walk into the darkness under the streetlight that made shadows on the trees and remember Harry's Bar where you were once in love and everything was good and clean.

"*Y pues nada,*" you would say and put your arm around the woman, and you would forget the hunger for a little while. Then when it was much later and you were in bed and you would turn to her and it was very good and you would smile and call her your little éclair, "*eclara mía,*" and she would look at you and tell that she was not a dessert tray. Later she would bring you a bottle and you would twist the cork until it popped under pressure and you would think how much like a cork some men are and you would know that you had opened the bottle well.

You would think about the champagne that they served at Harry's and wish that you could be there and sit in the corner table and laugh with the waiters. You remember how you would drink in the morning, and in the afternoon the bullfighters would arrive by plane and you would drink some more and in the evening your friends would gather and drink and you would would drink until morning, when you could start again. Then you would mix a tomato daiquiri for the hangover and you would read your notes, and you would remember when the woman stood up and laughed that you were all a sauced generation but you see that you had written it wrong. But then you smiled and the way it was written on the page was clear and true, and slowly you raised the pencil and the fire started inside and you began to write.

—*Chris McCarthy*

For Whom the Bear Tolls
or, The Old Man and Nan-Sea

▶ ▶ ▶ ▶ ▶ *I* looked at the pictures of Lincoln and Jefferson and Nixon, and I wondered why I couldn't be like them. But I knew that the people liked me, and that was good, because I really didn't do anything, so I needed them to like me.

"Ron, darling," Nancy said. "Come to bed now."

"Yes," I said. "But you know I really can't do anything?"

"Yes, but that's all right, because I love you anyway. We all do."

I lay in bed and thought about the Bear that was the Russian horde, trying to take over the world. I thought how damn annoying that Bear could be and how good it would be to get rid of it. But I was tired, so I went to sleep. I rose with the sun, and I went outside to look at my ranch. I wanted to see my bulls, but they were far away, and I didn't see a taxi. It began to rain, and that was bad, because I needed to practice my horseback riding to show the people I really could do something. I was getting wet, so I went back inside. It was the moment of truth. I needed to call my friends to talk about that damn Bear before I completely forgot about it.

Cap and Don and Bill and the two Georges arrived by taxi. "Let's have a drink, chaps," the better of the two Georges said.

I took out a bottle of champagne, and we drank. We drank some more, and I forgot to tell my friends my plan to skin the Bear, so we talked about our other friends who were the Contras and really rather nice chaps but not really one of us. They were not that interesting, so we began to get bored and had another drink.

"It would be nice if they went away," George said.

"The Contras?"

"No."

"Who?"

"Those damn Democrats! Those asses!" he said.

"Yes." George had never liked the Donkeys, ever since he began thinking about running for president.

"Wouldn't it be nice to get one of them in the ring."

"Quite." I wasn't sure whether he meant boxing or rodeo or bullfighting, but I didn't ask. He often got emotional when he drank, and it was best just to agree with him. Besides, I had forgotten what we were talking about.

"You know, Ron," the other George (who always behaved badly when he was drinking) said, "we really should think about it."

"What?"

"A freeze." He really was tight.

"You know I will never be able to say 'farewell to arms'?"

"Yes."

Nancy came in and looked at me and at my friends and back at me.

"What are you doing, dear?"

"I was talking with the chaps. Foreign policy."

"What rot. You're behaving rather badly. You know you can't make important decisions, dear."

"Yes, I know," I said. She was such a bitch sometimes. I heard her talking to my friends, and I wondered how come I couldn't be as smart as she was and tell my friends what to do. But I was thirsty, so I went outside, and I found a taxi. I told the driver to take me to Harry's Bar & American Grill. He did. It was still raining, and that was bad, because I couldn't sit outside at the tables and make jokes and drink and watch the stars, so I went inside. The bartender gave me a glass of Pernod. He was nice.

"Those damn Commies," I said. "If only I were as smart as Nancy, then I would know what to do."

"Of course," he said. He was very nice.

"I could have been such a fine president."

"Yes," he said. *"C'est la vie."*

I told him I didn't understand Spanish and paid him for the drink. I went out and left the bar and walked back to the ranch in the rain.

—*John McPartland*

MEN WITHOUT DRIVES

▶ ▶ ▶ ▶ ▶ *I*t was a good writing machine. But they would not let him take it into Harry's. The machine was brown like the young bull. The machine did not have horns. This machine would not prick you. The pencils would prick you but not the machine. They would allow pencils in Harry's. The pencils were good, too, but the machine was better. Even with all the wires the machine was better. He liked to sharpen pencils, but that was in the past. Sometimes he thought of the shavings curling into a white saucer and became sad. To hell with pencils. The machine had three pronged plugs and used short words like *load* and *save*. This was very good. But Harry's Bar & American Grill had only two-hole receptacles.

The room was cold now, and he opened the small stove and fed in five number-two Ticonderogas. The flames licked the rubber nipples of the pencils. He thought of his first three wives, of Brett, of the injury.

"I'm going out to load a drink," he said.

"Take your machine," she said.

"Do not be sharp," he said.

She said, "At least the machine plugs in."

"Do not save that thought," he said.

"The pencils were hard," she said.

He did not want to face her. In Pamplona they had drunk a very cold bottle of Moët & Chandon at the zinc bar. There he had whittled his instrument to a fine hard point. It had been very good then, but that was a long time off. Before the accident. Before the machine. There had been too many bottles of fine cold champagne since then. He wanted to cry.

"I am going out now," he said.

"I am happy you have the machine," she said.

"There are too many wires attached," he said.

"I wish there were more than floppy disks," she said.

"Yes, that is the truth," he said.

It was cold now, and he opened the door of the small stove and fed all but one of the pencils into the small cold flames. With his knife he sharpened the pencil. Small wood curls jumped to the floor. When the pencil was sharp, he pricked himself. The blood was red and fine. Then he threw the pencil into the flames.

"We could share a cab," she said. "Maybe I could help with the wires," she said. "They won't mind at Harry's," she said.

"No," he said. "This program is over."

—Kenneth McMurtry

THEN OF COURSE THERE
WAS THE LONG WINTER

▸ ▸ ▸ ▸ ▸ *T*hen of course there was the long winter in Zaragoza when he played much Pac-Man. The *Café
de las Siete-Once* was warm and clean, and the machines
were well-lighted, and they were not out of order like the
ones in the cafés controlled by the fascists.

Dick Jordan could hear the afternoon gunfire in the plaza
now as he played, moving quickly and fluidly through the
lanes of the maze, the absinthe burning in his fingers and
the one finger itching inside the cast, and the itching was
uncomfortable, but he did not let it affect his playing. He
worked the controls cleanly and well, with no exaggeration
of movement, and the stick felt good in his hand.

The machine was good, Dick thought, the way it would
be at Harry's Bar if Harry's had Pac-Man, but then you did
not need Pac-Man at Harry's because at Harry's you found
everything, and it was for the *Lombata di Vitello* and all the
other things that Dick Jordan wished he was at Harry's
now, but now there was only the war, and on his days off
he played Pac-Man.

He saw her at the Donkey Kong machine. She was young
and clean and amply built, and she carried a carbine. Her

skin was the color of whole wheat bread, and she had not shaved her left leg, as was the guerrilla symbol.

"Thou art the *inglés* of the Pac-Man, yes?" she said to Dick Jordan. "The manner of thy playing is that of one with the *huevos grandes*." She gestured with her hands, as if weighing cantaloupes.

"And thou, *camarada*, thou gave thy machine but one coin." Dick Jordan returned the compliment.

She touched his finger. "The fascists, no?"

"Yes," he said. "A tank."

"I obscenity myself in the putrid milk of this finger-fouling fascist tank," she said, and the words sounded beautiful in Spanish, and then she played Donkey Kong.

The girl's playing was reckless for a woman, Dick Jordan thought, but she took the barrels gracefully and well, and she did not go for the hammer too soon, and Dick liked this, and he also liked the way she held the stick.

Now the barrels were rolling fast and close, and she waited for the gap, the moment to climb the ladder. The girl stood her ground and leaped the barrels one at a time and the fireballs roared past her on both sides. Then the gap came.

"Take it now, little heifer," Dick Jordan said, and he saw the girl running for the ladder at full speed and then overshooting it and coming back, and now the barrel was too close, and Dick saw that her head would be crushed before she could top the ladder.

He grabbed her hand, pulling her back down, and there was the rush of air as the big barrel rolled past above her, and then she climbed up and took two more barrels and then another ladder, and then she was at the top, and it was finished, and the girl was holding on to Dick, her cartridge belt lumpy and hard against him, hard between the soft, ample breasts against his stomach, soft and then hard between and then soft, the buttocks ample and soft under the hard cast on his finger, and she smelled of the sea and pimientos and WD-40.

"I had much fear," she said, and Dick Jordan felt the buttocks flex, and then he felt her hand on his own buttocks, and he did not move the hand away.

"Thou played well, little obscenity," he said. "Truly, thou played bravely and well, and thou art my little unspeakable of the *huevos grandes* also, and someday I will take thee to Harry's, but first thou must shave both thy legs."

—Ken Bash

CHAPTER I

▸ ▸ ▸ ▸ ▸ *I*n the spring of that year the road came down from the mountain. The road was white and dry from the chalky soil, and white dust covered the leaves of the trees. Snow still guarded the peaks of the mountain, and it was rumored that the whiteness hid the carcasses of many leopards. No one asked why.

There were no soldiers here, so they did not march up the white road to the mountain. There were many Italians here, but few were ambulance drivers, and many drank wine from wineskins. Some drank the wine from bottles and some from wineglasses. The people drank all the time even if they were not Italian. All of them remembered the warmth of the milky white absinthe at Harry's Bar & American Grill, but that was in another country.

There were many cows here but no bulls. "I respect this place," Nick said. "It is an honest place." Nick entered the bodega to have a drink. It was clean and well-lighted. He felt good. The wine was good. This place could be the capital of the world, he thought.

He was right, of course. The place was always beautiful, unless in the middle of a four-day blow. The fathers and sons of Nick's family had lived here for many years. There was once an Indian camp near the river, and across the river and into the trees were green hills. When Nick was a kid, he would pretend to be in Africa. Once, moonstruck with an Indian girl, he had carved two big hearts in one of the pine trees.

Each day the sun would rise, and each evening it would go down. In the evenings the bell would toll as if in a farewell to the charms of the day.

One day a gambler and a nun came into town and told how they had heard on the radio about the killers. Nick was not afraid. He knew that a killer was a way he would never be. Not even if he was an old man or lost at sea. There was a death that afternoon, and Nick was sorry. He wanted to run. He thought it would be good to escape to an island in a stream—to be in a Garden of Eden. This had been a dangerous summer. The feasts had been immoveable, and although he wanted to have, he had not.

—Walter John Hickey

In Those Days

▶ ▶ ▶ ▶ ▶ *I*n those days I used to write on the cockfights and the head knockers down around the bad section of town on the avenues off of the rue Prostitutée. You had to dry shave with a sickle just to get into those places, and I went, and they knew me. We were dangerous men in a dangerous time, but it was all we had in those days.

Then the steaks were big and juicy, and you had to bring your own sickle to cut the legs off, but they were rare and good with a tinge of skin for color and something to chew after you were done.

There were steaks like that in other places too, and they were places I liked. Harry's in Florence was one of the best. Harry's was clean though and good, and any aficionado who was an aficionado went there to eat and shoot the bull. There was wine there too, good wine, and during the war the men stationed in the unit outside of town used to drive down from the ridge in the snow in their drunk tank and drink and raise hell and beat the Italian busboys like they were their wives. Then the police would come and beat the soldiers like they were their wives and haul them all off to jail. The Italian busboys had no one to beat, so they beat their dogs like they were dogs and drank wine and tried to forget they were Italian busboys. They were tough men in a tough time, but that was long ago in a faraway place.

One night I was down on the avenues and the fights were scheduled, and the first fight of the night was beginning, but it was across the bar at a dinner table where a steak had jumped off a plate, and two men shot it and were each pulling on a leg and arguing over who would eat it.

"Leggo ma steako," growled the burly one in dialect Italian.

"Leggo MA steako," said the other and reached for his sickle and would have shaved the burly one if the bartender hadn't driven over a new steak to keep the peace.

It was wet outside and tough inside and cold all over, and the fights were about to start. It was a good time if you could afford your own sickle.

The first head knocker beat his man in the first round and then started beating on one of the steers who was yelling that the fight was fixed. The night was going to be a tough one, and cold inside and wet all over, but in those days that's what it was to be a man in a country that fought the bull instead of stabbing at it with fancy steak knives.

In the end the first fighter lay gored in the ring not moving. The steer went home that night after a beer and a pat on the rump from the men.

It was tough in those days, but I had a sickle and a nickel

in my pocket, and that was good. It was good to be dangerous and dangerous to be good. It was good to be bad. I was bad, and that was good. It's good to be good, but I was bad and dangerous, and that was good in those days.

—Patrick Moser

We Came Up Out of the
Valley into Sepulveda Pass

▶ ▶ ▶ ▶ ▶ *W*e came up out of the valley into Sepulveda Pass just before noon. Jack Wright was driving. Jack Wright was once the heavyweight champion of Van Nuys, but twenty years of hard living and one hundred thousand liters of cognac showed in his face when the light was right. We decided to lunch at Harry's. The thrushes were singing, and with all the traffic I never heard a single one of them.

The city was like a tall, graceful woman at this time of day. The people here decided long ago not to have a bus service and not to build a metro and not to have a train service and not to run a passenger balloon service so that they could retain the right to drive their own cars. So for ten months of the year, when the sun was high enough, you could see this wonderful blue-gray haze that hung over the city and made the trees look distant and defiant. Trees breathe in bad air and breathe out good air, which made these trees the healthiest trees in all the world.

We had hit the pass at a good time. If you hit the pass at a bad time, you can read *Huckleberry Finn* between the Galleria and Mulholland. But now at this good time Jack

Wright had us at the top in no time, and I looked back to see the great valley and the Santa Susanas, and the rich gray haze blotted out everything like a sophisticated woman entering a room.

Going very quickly, the motorcycle passed us. It was the tall kid with the skinny neck we had seen at breakfast in Camarillo. He lay forward over the bike the way John Surtees used to do at the Nurburgring. Seconds after the kid passed us the black-and-white police car with the orange and red lights flashing and the siren screaming passed us also.

Suddenly the kid soared aloft like an eagle, and we stopped with many others to look down onto Wilshire Boulevard. He had entered a concrete bridge abutment at great speed. The rear end of the bike and the kid's legs were all that protruded from the concrete. He was killed well.

—*Tom Maxwell*

IN THE SPRING HE TOOK THE
YOUNG WOMAN TO THE BAHAMAS

▶ ▶ ▶ ▶ ▶ *I*n the spring he took the young woman
to the Bahamas, avoiding the reporters and living on rum
and sun and the catch of the day and cruising on the mil-
lionaire's yacht. He had not taken his wife. His companion
gave him a feeling of invulnerability, that the plurality in
the fall, a year distant, would be his. This was truly a gift:
time and the talent for eluding the newsmen and spiritual
purity.

He remembered the words of Warren, who had called
from his cellular car phone and said, "Truly, Gary, you can
be president and none will oppose you."

"But," he had replied, "this is not as I have heard it, and
times are not as good as those when we were sitting at our
table at Harry's Bar and tasting the spaghetti and drinking
wine."

"Pasta," Warren said, "remember they call it pasta."

Yes, pasta, he thought, aware of the young woman on
his lap and of his wife in Colorado. Such were the demands
of a politician. And what of the others? It was not Jackson
I will have to fight but Simon and Biden and Dukakis and
Gore. Poor Cuomo will never get nominated, and Gore's

wife hates rock and roll, and Biden has unoriginal thoughts, and Dukakis has a difficult name, like the one I left behind. And everyone thinks Simon wrote "Mrs. Robinson."

But I must wage a campaign and shake a hundred thousand hands and pitch my book. The agent has said it is a fine book, one worthy of Arthur Schlesinger or Elmore Leonard or Stephen King, all invulnerable. And I must face the media hordes with my chin upraised and eyes on the horizon, mustn't I?

"So take the photo now," he said. "It may be an Instamatic photo, but the day is short and the weather good, and the photo will be enough. Nobody will see it, and nobody will know we were here, and in the morning when the warm rain falls, we will return to Washington, and in the fall we will meet again." I will tell the reporters, he thought, that they can follow me if they want, because I have nothing to hide and nothing to be ashamed of, though I wish the fall were here today.

He could feel the softness of the young woman on his lap and the sunlight glare in his eyes and the dizziness from the rum. What the hell, he thought, Warren said everything would be okay. Time for some fishing.

—Stanley Moss

For Whom the Rope Soles

▶ ▶ ▶ ▶ ▶ *P*apa saw the paper, and he saw the words on the paper, and he knew that it was a translation. Here at the corner table in Harry's Bar & American Grill he knew it was so.

"It is a translation," said the girl with the legs that were shaved.

"Truly," he said, and he thought of the girl, and he thought of the paper, and he thought of her legs, and the ache came back into his throat. It was the ache of the deep indigestion or maybe of the heartburn. He did not know what it was. It was always something.

"Tell me it is good even if it is not very good," she said.

"I will tell you how it is, daughter," he said, and he ran his hand over her right leg.

"Papa, tell me it is good and that someday I will know all the tenses and know of the irregular verbs and even of the little words that sometimes end with *o* and other times end with *a*, and we will be happy."

"Someday you will know it, my little rodent," he said, and the heartburn was suddenly big in his throat.

"I will even know what it said in the *tendidos* when the *toreando* is very bad?" asked the girl, and her ears were pink and fluted like the mollusks of the Guadalquivir.

"Even so," he said, "and we will conjugate together."

"Is it good?" she said.

"Yes," he said briefly.

"The translation?" she asked.

"The leg," he said.

He knew the meaning of the words that were said in the *tendidos*. The words that came quick and hard and bitter when the *toreando* had no purity and the sword sank into the sweetbreads and there was no *cargando la suerte*. He knew the words. He knew Spanish.

"You will know them, daughter," he said. "You will know them, and it will be a fine thing that you know them."

"Perhaps I will even know it so that my words will be of clear green and of muleta red? The words will be like a wounded fawn seeking the refuge of the forest?" she asked.

"*Guantanamera*," muttered the *mujer* of Pablo from the shadows. "*Guajira, guantanamera.*"

"Shut up, Pilar," he said, not unkindly.

" ———— ," said Pilar, saying nothing.

"Go," he said to the girl, "and conjugate quickly those verbs that must be conjugated."

"Okeydokey," she said in her deep Cordoban accent. "But I do not know how. Where do the noses go?"

"This stuff is harder to write than you thought," he said, "Is it not?"

And then suddenly he knew, and then they both knew.

They knew that it was time for dinner, for that is why the waiter had brought it, and he had done it well and true, using a tray.

—*Patricia Brodin Oen*

ONCE, WHEN HE COULD NO LONGER BOX

▸ ▸ ▸ ▸ ▸ Once, when he could no longer box, he became a cook. It was good to be a cook. In the winter the stoves were hot, and in the summer the stoves were still hot, but the beer was cold. Besides, if you were lucky, there was fish. We liked to eat the fish by the machine for dishes and talk of the boxers.

"He is not such a good boxer, only he is strong," Harry said.

He finished his fish and took some beer. "This is good, no?"

"Yes, this is fine," I said.

"And he will be the champion."

"Like you."

He laughed and went quiet and said, "You are a friend." I went back to the machine. The noise came and the steam, and I could see Harry by the board for chopping. He had big hands and chopped with speed. I thought how fast he was as a boxer, before everything went sour in the Garden at his last fight. It was against a Mexican. Harry said that Mexicans made the best boxers because they were brave.

Always, when the customers were not there any longer, I cleaned the grill, and when I was done, Harry and I could go to the bar. Sometimes there would be women, and they wore cotton dresses in the summer, and when a breeze blew, you could see above their knees, and it was fine to think of them, but mostly we talked of the boxers and who was a good champion at this. Afterward, after many beers, Harry would be in despair, and it made him too bitter to talk of the ring, so we would talk of dreams. There were many dreams now.

"Someday I will have my own place."

"How will it be?"

"Clean and there will be lights."

"And windows?"

"Yes, because windows are good for sitting in the afternoon with a good beer and a friend."

"And the food?"

"The food will be good and simple, food for champions."

"And the walls, Harry?"

"The walls will have photos of many old champions, and some will be new."

"And will there be a sign?"

"Yes, there must be a sign."

Then, after a while, Harry didn't come anymore, and I would wait by the machine with its noise and the steam. And after a time I didn't think of Harry anymore. Only sometimes I wondered if he got the sign I knew he wanted: Harry's Bar & American Grill—Good Food and Good Friends.

—*Theo Pelletier*

"THINK YOU'LL ENTER?" NICK ASKED

▶ ▶ ▶ ▶ ▶ *T*hink you'll enter?" Nick asked.

"Chance of it," she said and smiled.

"Want to try?"

"Sure."

"Was it Africa?"

"No."

They ate the bacon and eggs and drank the wine.

"Not Harry's? You said you loved it there."

"I know."

"Florence?"

"Sure."

They sat there smoking. An old man came and took away the plates.

"When will you know?" Nick asked.

"Soon."

"It's hell, isn't it?" Nick said.

"Contests always make me feel this way," she said.

"Feel bad?" Nick asked.

"No, I feel good but funny."

"I know. The bastards."

"I don't want to quarrel. Let's not quarrel. Maybe an idea will come. Maybe an idea will come today."

"Really?"

"Isn't that lovely?"

"I don't know."

"That's the way it is with contests."

"Yes," Nick said.

"Florence is fine."

"It's swell."

—*Doris Cruze*

THE SNOWS ALSO FALL

► ► ► ► ► *T*he Americans had been very brave but very stupid. Now there were small huddles on the stones of the plaza. There were flies. Small green ones. He didn't like small green ones.

The English had been very, very brave but not as smart as the Americans.

The Norwegians were almost as smart as the English, but they always went in in a clean line. Never in quite the right direction, but the line was clean and true and straight. But direction was nada. Going in straight was not nada; Hans, the Norwegian, had said.

Hans had gone in very straight over the edge of the plaza. It had been a good, true fall. Until the splat. But the splat was nada.

Going into Harry's Bar & American Grill had always been good. The true, quick turn from the sidewalk. The hard, precise, straight arm push right on the *a* in *bar*. The moment of truth as the door went past your nose. That was a true moment.

Sometimes you were off-center of the *a*, and the door

did not swing past your nose, and that was true also. Not good, but true.

Some true things are truer than other true things. Hans, the Norwegian, had always said things like that. Perhaps the splat had not been nada.

Anna, the Anatolian, stirred next to him as she made ready. He reached over and patted the top of her small, fuzzy head.

"Go with God, little rabbit."

"Obscenity thee," she said shyly. She always said that before she went in.

Anna was clever and brave. She lasted longer than the Americans, but not as long as the Serbo-Croatians.

Now it was his turn. Sometimes when an old man wanted to say farewell to arms, he had to go over the trees to get to the big, two-hearted river.

The dark came down, and he could smell the pine needles. The light glinted off the snow of the green hills as the earth moved under him.

It had been a short, happy life, and he had always gone in straight. The last thing he heard was the bell tolling.

Going in straight had not been nada. He wished he had Hans around to explain that to him again.

—*Dominick P. Scotto*

The Old Man and the P.C.

▶ ▶ ▶ ▶ ▶ *H*e was an old man, and he played alone, and he played hard and good, and he could beat any game in the video arcade. He worked the joystick and pressed the fire button, and he zapped the asteroids and UFOs and aliens, and gobbled monsters and ran the scores up until the numbers ran out and started at zero again, and he was the fastest quark laser in the West. Then one day he went home and left his fans behind, the men and boys who all loved him and the women and girls who all loved him too and wanted him to father their children. And he hooked up the personal-computer hardware to his television set, and he played hard and good, and he played alone until the day that *she* showed up at his front door, and she was not the Avon lady. She was tall and slim and straight and good to look at and had legs that went all the way up to Mount Kilimanjaro, and she asked the tough questions.

"Old man, why do you waste your time playing video games? You who were the good fisherman who went beyond the deep well of the gulf and caught the truly great fish."

"Obscenity on that fish!" he snorted. "By the time I got the fish on land the sharks were picking their teeth with his bones. I had a skeleton of the fish that was, and the people they all laughed at me, and I had to open a can of tuna fish for my supper. So no more fishing for me! My whole life was just stupid symbolism anyway. And now I stay at home and chase all the symbols I want and catch the big one right here on my tv set."

"And when you have beaten all the arcade and home video games, then what?"

"Then I slip in the word-processor software, and write the good and true sentences about my symbolic life, the days at the sidewalk cafés in Paris talking the boring talk with American and British drunks and never once going to the Eiffel Tower or to the Louvre, and the fine and good days of love and war in Spain when you couldn't tell the difference between a Communist and an Antifascist without a manifesto, and the truly good days at Harry's Bar & American Grill in Florence, where you could always get a truly dry martini and combination pizza, hold the anchovies, and other spicy Italian dishes with truly great legs who all wanted me to father their children. And I drop names like Scott Fitzgerald and James Joyce and Ezra Pound and also Gertrude Stein, who was the world's greatest cryptographer—even the computers cannot decipher her writing—and Gertrude's companion, Alice, who had a better mustache than I, and neither of them wanted me to father their children. I put the word processor on automatic pilot, and it gets the words right and writes true and good sentences and plugs in an *and* every three words all by itself. And the personal computer has revealed to me the greatest of the universal truths: Garbage in, Garbage out."

"Old man, I don't know RAM from a ROM, and *software incompatibility* means impotence as grounds for divorce, as far as I'm concerned, but I do know that I have a game you can't beat. It's called Love & Sex in the Universe. Do you know the difference between love and sex?"

"Sure. Sex is never having to say you're Ernest. And there is not any game that I cannot beat. I am *campeón*, and they say that I have the moves and reflexes of a ballet dancer or a bullfighter."

"Look, old man, the only similarity between you and a bullfighter or ballet dancer is the wad of socks you have stuffed in your jockey shorts. Let's play!"

She grabbed his joystick, and the game was on. She zapped and he zapped and they both zapped together, and she scored and he scored and they both scored together, and she and he became they and you became thee and thee for me and tea for two and two for tea and they'd rather swing on a star and then they zoomed into hyperspace and through the black hole into nowhere that was a truly great nowhere, and then the universe moved and the printed circuits melted and the pixels pulled apart and the picture tube blew and the TV screen faded to black.

"Olé! Thou swell!" she cried. "You were right, old man. You are truly state-of-the art! Adiós, *campeón*. Keep your joystick up."

VOLUME II

But the old man did not hear. He was sleeping, and he was dreaming about space invaders with truly great legs who wanted him to father their children.

—Jack Schmidt

THE CAFÉ KILLED BILL MANJARO

▶ ▶ ▶ ▶ ▶ *T*he Beverly Center is a snow-covered shopping mall in California. At 19,710 feet, it is said to be the highest shopping mall in the state. But then, no one really cares how tall a building is. Close to the roof, however high that is, is the dried and frozen remains of a Girl Scout. No one has explained why anyone would try to sell cookies at that altitude.

"You know, the marvelous thing is that it's painless," he said. "That's how you know when it starts."

"Is it really?"

"Absolutely. I'm really sorry about the odor, though. That must bother you."

"No, not really," she replied. "I just thought it was rather bad to be trapped in a school cafeteria."

"It's not so bad. I've gotten used to the indigestion and the food poisoning. So it's not so bad," replied Bill Manjaro.

"Please tell me what I can do. There must be something I can do."

"You could stop the feeding of iguana meat and shoe leather to innocent students, or you could shoot me."

"Why would I shoot you?"

"I don't know. Because you know how, I guess."

The woman leaned back against the refrigerator-freezer. She looked tired and worn and dirty from crawling around near the cookie ovens and ice-making machines. "I wish we'd never come, Bill," she said.

He thought back to the happy days he'd had. Life selling carnations at the airport had been good. It had been very good. It had been as good as a cold beer on a hot day in Pamplona during the summer in bullfighting season on a Sunday afternoon at the café down the short road to Harry's Bar & American Grill. He would never write about it now.

"Someone will come," said the woman.

"How will they know we're here?"

"Maybe they'll smell us," she suggested hopefully.

"No one ever smells anything here," he replied.

The teacher stood at the desk in the front of the room. He was tall and thin and old and had a twitch. He talked.

Bill, who sat at the desk on the side of the room, listened. He tried to listen. Bill listened. But not really. It was like when you taste a beer but can't tell if it's good because it's so cold.

The teacher was still talking. No one listened. He was like a bad talk show host, only you couldn't turn him off. The teacher twitched.

The fluorescent light hummed like the sound of a crowd at a bullfight in a ring at Pamplona on a hot afternoon. The bell rang. The class sighed. A drink would be good, thought Bill.

Nick, who was short and looked tired, walked over to Bill.
"Wanna go?" asked Nick.
"Where?"
"To the cafeteria."
"Why?"
"Because that's what we always do," replied Nick.
"That'd be killer," answered Bill as he stood up from the desk.

He could feel death sitting on his chest like a dead bull in Pamplona on a hot afternoon. Then he was flying over the shopping mall. He saw the Hard Rock Café and knew where he was going. The Beverly Center shone brightly in the smog.

—*Cindy Tobisman*

ROBERT JORDAN RIVERS LAY
WITH THE GIRL

▶ ▶ ▶ ▶ ▶ *R*obert Jordan Rivers lay with the girl as he watched the fire. He could see Pilaf and Pablum preparing the evening meal of liver, peas, and Spanish rice. He pondered as to why a rich American like Robert Jordan Rivers would help fight a war that was not his concern. He did not know why. He thought about spring and the many trout streams at home. Torrance, where the young loins run on the beaches. He thought about bygone university days and the countless good times spent consuming garlic and absinthe at Harry's Bar & American Grill. Yes, he thought, nothing could equal Torrance in the spring. The thought was broken when Murine awoke.

And she said, "I'm awake. It is good to be awake with thee."

"You are like a callow animal," said Robert Jordan Rivers. "You are like a small deer or foal. Shall I call thee filly?"

"Nay."

"Then I shall call thee fawn. Will fawn do?"

"Yes."

"Let us rise, fawn."

"Thou art hungry," she said.

Pablum stirred. "*Inglés,* tomorrow we will kill many of the guardia civil and spread their entrails over the country-side," he said.

"The morning and the spreading of entrails will come soon enough," said Pilaf.

"First let us eat."

Pilaf knelt down to serve the food. Pablum served the grenades, automatic rifles, and captured Mausers. Robert Jordan Rivers picked up the fork, holding it carefully so that the peas would not roll onto the floor of the dark cave.

"Thou art a good friend," Pilaf said. "Thou canst eat like a Fascist pig." It was then that Robert Jordan Rivers knew that Pilaf was a friend. Murine looked directly at him. When she peered over the liver and into the peas, Robert Jordan Rivers knew his destiny.

Pilaf smiled. "*Inglés,* the eyes of war are for many," she said, "but Murine is for your eyes only."

He smiled and resumed his meal. It was a side of Pilaf that Robert Jordan Rivers had never seen before.

—*John C. Toth*

A Private Conversation in Harry's Bar

▶ ▶ ▶ ▶ ▶ *A*fter the shooting of the ducks in the fall of that year, before the big snow, with true whiteness and with a silence as of the death of goldfish, fell on the bare-assed mountains and into the trees across the river, he arrived in Venice at 17:03 military time and checked into the Gritti Hotel where she was waiting in the bar. Christ he loved her for her heartbreak face, and she loved him for his famous wounds.

He was a general in the U.S. National Guard, with many true and famous wounds, and he was one beat-up son of a bitch with true handles and to hell with the pain. He was fifty-nine years old, and his truest and Most Wonderful Wound, which everyone in this town knew about, loved, and truly respected, but no one mentioned, knowing silently and with true certainty, was located directly behind his fly. That was one hell of a wound, but we don't talk about that, do we, boy, General, sir, and how do you like it now, gentlemen?

The lady waiting in the bar was a true Princessa of this town, fifteen years of age and true jailbait, with the heart-break face and truly descended from the condottieri, who damn well knew how to defend this town when the chips were down. She loved all of his wounds well and truly but most especially his Most Wonderful Wound directly behind his fly, which in her opinion was the most aristocratic of his wounds, if a wound may truly be called aristocratic and if you are judging wounds fairly and impartially by the standards of this town.

"Let's go to Harry's Bar & American Grill," said the general, "and look at the famous writers and the rich war profiteers and the big international whores."

"Yes," said the Princessa. "Yes. Yes. Yes."

They sat in Harry's Bar and looked at the overly famous writers, the aging film stars, and the goddamn tourists who should have stayed the hell in Missoula, Montana. They also observed a number of overaged bullfighters of the loud mouth and seventeen world-class whores en route to St. Moritz.

"Is it perhaps of some interest, the environment?" asked the general.

"It is truly awesome," said the Princessa. "One feels the drama, the emotion, the weltschmerz."

"Weltschmerz me no weltschmerz," said the general. "That's an order."

"I truly regret the error of the weltschmerz. However, it was not necessary to bring on the authority of the five stars, General, sir."

"I regret the being of the bastard. Eff the heavy artillery. Let us now resume the monumental having of the fun."

"It is resumed. The fiesta continues as before the bombardment of the civilians."

He poured the champagne and spoke as gently as one used to command can, not wishing to command.

"Daughter."

"Papa."

"Oh you of the heartbreak face."

"Oh you of the famous wounds."

"Let us drink to all true jailbait, foreign and domestic, and also to you, you thrice lovely jailbait you, and to hell with the pain."

"Yes. Yes. Let us also drink to the five sons we will never have, who will never become famous condottieri and will never defend this town when the chips are truly down, due to your unfortunate and truly famous wounds."

"To the goddamn missing sons, five in number, by the number, in numerical order."

"To the famous and at times truly inconvenient wounds."

"To death and all crummy bastards, whenever and wherever," he said, riding the pain which to hell with.

"To various crummy bastards."

"To this most famous and satisfactory of bistros." He smiled for the first time in fifty-three years.

"To Harry's Bar."

They drank. Christ he loved her for her heartbreak face. And she loved him well and truly and fully and finally and once and for all for his truly famous wounds and most of all for his Most Wonderful Wound located immediately behind his fly.

—Kenneth C. Dyches

SHE HAD TOLD HIM TO
MEET HER AT HARRY'S BAR

▶ ▶ ▶ ▶ ▶ She had told him to meet her at Harry's Bar, but she didn't tell him which one. That was not good. He would wait for her here in Kansas at the bodega at the foot of the mountain. He knew her. If she were to come, she would come this way. He would wait.

That last day she had wanted to take the veil.

"I want to take the veil," she said.

That was after the thing in the bullring. "No," he had called to her, "the other end. An ear! An ear!" She had brought it back with her in a sack to Harry's, a long way from that bullring.

"It's big, isn't it, darling?" She showed it to him.

It had ripened. Maybe she should take the veil, he thought then.

It would be good later, if she came. He pulled the flask from his hip pocket. He pulled the cork and drank. Luigi would have liked that, that he had remembered, remembered to pull out the cork. It started to rain.

It was getting dark and colder. He stood and walked over to the edge of the waterfall. He let the remaining drops of brandy fall into the stream below, to the trout swimming downstream to spawn. Yes, it would be good later if she came.

He went back to the bodega. She wasn't there, and there was no message. "Your friend no come?" asked the barman, wiping the counter with a greasy rag. The smell didn't cover the garlic on his breath. "We close now." The barman put out the lights.

He left the bodega and walked home in the rain.

—*Irving Warnasch*

HE COULD FEEL THE STEADY HARD PULL

▶ ▶ ▶ ▶ ▶ *He* could feel the steady hard pull, and his left hand was cramped. It drew up tight, and he looked at it in disgust. "I wish I had the boy," he said. "To help me and to see this." "What kind of a hand is that," he said. "Cramp then if you want. Make yourself into a claw. It will do you no good." If the boy were here, he could rub it for me and loosen it down from the forearm, he thought. But it will loosen up. The old man was wet with sweat and tired deep into his bones. "But you have not slept yet, old man," he said aloud. "It is half a day and a night and now another day, and you have not slept." For an hour the old man had been seeing black spots before his eyes. He was not afraid of the black spots. They were normal, though twice he had felt faint and dizzy, and that had worried him. I'm clear enough in the head, he thought.

Then the old man looked up and saw how large it was. The old man had seen many large ones before. He had two large ones in his life, but never alone. Now alone, he was fast to the largest he had even seen and bigger than he had ever heard of, and his left hand was still tight as the gripped claws of an eagle. "I am not religious," he said. "But I will say ten Our Fathers and ten Hail Marys that I should win this one, and I promise to make a pilgrimage to the Virgin if I do. That is a promise."

Perhaps I should not do this, he thought. But this is the thing I was born for. He thought how he had come to understand his opponent over time. He knew when he would dive, when he would disappear and when he would come up. The old man would respond to each change of direction by pulling back, leaning forward, or shifting his weight, being careful not to jerk. He had great respect for his opponent. But I will show him what a man can do and what a man endures.

Then the old man looked up, and he knew that it was over. He slowly released his cramped hand from the joystick. He saw that he had tallied more points than anyone ever had. He put his hands in his pockets but found he had no more quarters with which to play. He turned and walked out of the door of Harry's Bar & American Grill.

Later the old man was sleeping on his face, and the boy was sitting by watching him. The old man was dreaming about Pac Man.

—*Roberta Faeth Slaski*

IT WAS THE MIDDLE OF THE AFTERNOON

▶ ▶ ▶ ▶ ▶ *I*t was the middle of the afternoon, and the beach was very hot. The young man slept in the shadows of a palm. A piece of flat, hard bread stuffed with goat cheese was wrapped in newspapers and half buried in the sand. A rooster pecked nearby. It touched the food and stopped when it reached the man's face.

He woke and saw the rooster looking him in the eye. It was old. It had survived many cockfights and was featherless. It has lost all of its proud rooster things.

"Scram, you cretin!" He waved his arm and threw sand at the skinny bird.

He turned onto his stomach. The beach was empty, and it was white with the heat. He fell asleep again.

He lit the woman's cigarette. She smiled and looked outside at the rain. He drank the vintage cabernet. The restaurant was alive. People were laughing. The woman removed her gloves and stacked them carefully alongside the ashtray. She had beautiful hands. He felt very self-conscious. He was sure he didn't know her. So he read the matches: Harry's Bar & American Grill. The club was suddenly silent. Everyone was looking at them.

"Where are we?" he asked the woman.

"Welcome to Harry's," she spoke softly, and her hands opened to include the room. "I am the storyteller." The patrons cheered. Glasses were raised. He stood up with the others and raised his glass to the mysterious woman.

"And tonight we begin with you." She looked the young man in the eye. Her beauty made him sweat. Everyone looked at him. The bartender smiled and gave him a wink. The waiters were still. They had been through this before.

"You are the story," the woman whispered into the young man's ear. She laughed and kissed him on the cheek. Her lips were hard. The kiss had a bite.

"Ouch!" He jumped up from the sand. The rooster was on his shoulder. He shoved it off. It flew to the middle of his back. Its claws dug into his skin. The rooster pecked the back of his neck. He screamed, and ran. He dove into the cool water. He went in deep and swam with the fish. When he could no longer feel the rooster or the scratches, he came to the surface.

The rooster stood on a rock in the middle of the water. It looked even bigger. He swam to shore. He looked for a stick. He wished he had a gun. He threw a rock at the rooster, and it landed short.

It was ugly. But it was only a chicken. It stood on the rock in the middle of the water. The young man returned to his shade. The sun was still high in the sky, and the afternoon was hot. The rooster watched the beach. It was empty. The young man was asleep. The rooster pecked at the rock.

The rooster was pissed off.

—*Beth Rehrer*

THE NEXT SENTENCE

▶ ▶ ▶ ▶ ▶ *T*he American wrote, *The hills across the valley of the Ebro were long and white.*

"It needs a lot of work," Jig said.

"Work?"

"It has too many words in it."

She was probably right. Or at least words with too many letters. Later he would go back and change *across* to *in* and *hills* to *hill.* He might even change *white* to *brown,* his favorite color. But now he had to go on to the next sentence. He wanted to stop for another beer. But it was getting late, and the last mail train this year was due in ten minutes.

He tried, *On this side there was no shade and no trees and the station was between two lines of rails in the sun.*

"It's hard to read. Put a comma after *shade* and *station* and a semicolon after *trees,*" Jig said.

He knew all the big punctuation marks. But he refused to use them. He had seen what it had done to his friends in London, Rome, and New York. Sentences you would never punctuate that way unless you were tired of war, women, and beer.

He thought about the next sentence. It had to be right. Something with *and, said,* and *you* in it.

"You need a footnote," Jig said.

"A footnote?"

"To tell the judges at Harry's Bar & American Grill how hard it was."

"Hard?"

"The next sentence and no time for another beer."

—*Gene and Mary Washington*

GIRL IN THE RAIN

▶ ▶ ▶ ▶ ▶ *G*eorge stood in the window looking across the patio. Rain dripped from the eaves of the hotel, blurring the sign for Harry's Bar & American Grill across the avenue. It drummed steadily on the dark bricks below and polished the bronze plaque commemorating World War II dead—the goddamn cold rain he's come all the way from Missouri to California to leave behind.

Two thousand miles and here he was stuck in the damn hotel room. His wife was stretched out on the bed with two pillows under her head. She was reading one of the books she'd brought along, happy as a kitten, he could tell—as though she'd planned this all along.

What was that he could see in the doorway next to Harry's? It had barely moved, but George saw that it was a girl with two long blond braids. She was huddled into a man's suit coat trying to make herself small enough to keep dry.

"I'm going down to get that girl," he said. "I'm going to take her to Harry's for a good, hot cup of coffee."

"How nice," his wife answered, never taking her eyes from the page. "Stay dry."

George went past the desk clerk with the bright red, teasing mouth. "Don't get wet." She smiled.

"There's a girl over there, down on her luck. I'm going to take her to Harry's for coffee."

"Wait, here's my umbrella," the red lips said, and there she was holding the umbrella high over George's head.

George skirted the puddles, reaching the doorway out of breath. The girl was gone. He looked to his right and then left past Harry's, but she was nowhere to be seen. Damn! Where had she got to? In a funk, George tramped back upstairs.

"Back so soon?" his wife asked. She hadn't moved from the bed.

"She was gone, disappeared," he replied. "Do you think I scared her away? I only wanted to help—she looked so cold. Do you think I looked threatening? Would you have been afraid?"

"No, dear George, you're so kind and gentle; how could anyone be frightened of you?"

Someone knocked at the door. "Come in," George called. There stood the bellboy with a girl; her eyes were cornflower blue, and one wet, blond braid, resting on her breast, rose and fell with her breathing. "Excuse me," he said, "the desk clerk said she was a friend of yours."

—*Juanita J. O'Connell*

It Was Hot in the Redwood Tub

▶ ▶ ▶ ▶ ▶ *I*t was hot in the redwood tub. The old man drank Perrier. The tub was too hot, but a man does not mind burns. The men who train the horses have a name for such water. They call it *agua caliente*.

To the west was the ocean. But today the old man could not see *la mar*, which is what people call her in Spanish when they love her, because of *el smog*.

It was quiet in the canyon. Soon the old man would watch the others. They would run in front of the bulldozers through the narrow canyon to the site of Pamplona Hills Estates to protest the building of the condominiums. But the old man did not care. There would be a bodega in the shopping center where the boy could buy tuna fish. And a Harry's Bar. Everyone would come to Harry's.

The boy came out to the deck. He had news about the football, about the Bowl of the Supers, as the players were called. "I have faith in the Rams of Los Angeles," the boy said.

"But they have left Los Angeles, my son," the old man replied. "They have gone to the city called Anaheim."

"I have heard of this Anaheim," said the boy. "But it is

not where the players of *fútbol* live. It is where the mouse called Mickey has a home."

The old man could not speak to him about the castle built by Disney and the new frontiers of football. He was seized by a great hunger.

"Bring me the usual breakfast," he told the boy. "Toast with butter and marmalade, a fried egg, and hot tea with sugar."

"Are these things not bad for you?" asked the boy. "The fats and the sugars. While you were away, a man died in the next canyon from such a diet."

"That is superstition. How do you know it wasn't just the whiskey?"

"No, señor. The doctors from the medical association—"

The old man cut him off. He was reading an article in the magazine that they had brought him about properties in the canyon. If I had bought some more land just two years ago, he thought. It was painful to read today of what had happened to the prices. Tomorrow he would feel the same, he knew. But on the fourth day, it would be all right.

—*Paula Ruth Van Gelder*

Nick Adams Stopped at
the End of the Aisle

▶ ▶ ▶ ▶ ▶ *N*ick Adams stopped at the end of the aisle. He leaned against the handle of his cart and wiped the sweat from his forehead. The cart was made of galvanized steel. It was a good cart. Nick looked beyond the macaroni and past the diet soft drinks and over the pyramid of oranges to where a white mist rose from the frozen foods. Bill was standing there, holding a can of frozen orange juice.

"You're holding a can of frozen orange juice," Nick said.

"Yes," Bill said. "Do you want to hold it?"

Nick took the can of frozen orange juice. His big hand went all the way around it. The can was cold.

"This can is cold," Nick said.

"Yes," Bill said. "That's the way it is here."

"Yes," Nick said. "That's the way it's been in every supermarket I've ever seen."

Nick put the orange juice into his cart. "What should we get next?" he asked.

"Gee," Bill said, "the apples look good."

Nick looked at the apples. "They look swell," he said.

Nick unrolled a plastic bag from the roll of plastic bags on the wall, pulling down on the bag, then tearing it cleanly and well along its perforations. He pulled open the mouth of the bag and held it in his left hand. With his right hand he picked up two apples and put them into the bag. Then he picked up another two apples and put them into the bag with the other apples.

"Is that enough apples?" Nick asked.

"I guess so," Bill said. "I guess it's enough apples."

Nick turned the cart toward the cash registers and got in one of the lines. The line was long.

"I wish I weren't here," Bill said.

"Where do you wish you were?" Nick asked.

"I wish I was at Harry's Bar," Bill said.

"Harry's Bar is a long way away," Nick said.

"It's so far away it's awful," Bill said.

"Well," said Nick, "you better not think about it."

—Geoffrey Wisner

IT WAS WINTER THEN

▶ ▶ ▶ ▶ ▶ *I*t was winter then, and the words came sweet and clean. Now it was spring and the words did not come, and she must enter the contest and win.

Every day the tall one with the thick muscles and tight pants called. His name was Charley, and he had been to Africa. He was a man all right.

"Come," he said to her. "We will drink wine and dance hotly and after make love hotlier in the hot tub."

"No," she told him. "I am cold with the fear of losing. Italy is old and fine, and the wine is red and warm. Here the wine is pale and chilled, and I obscenity on it and in it and your hot tub too."

"You are a good blond, but you lack all sanity," said Charley, not knowing what she was talking about and not caring to ask for there was one thing on his mind only.

In her life she had been strong and needed no makeup. Now she was weak, and there were pink spots on her face like tender buds on the magnolia trees that bloomed lovingly in the spring. She had broken out.

She sat and looked at the paper as though she had never seen paper before. She got up. She cleaned the windows and watched the sparrows fly out of the tile roof next door. She took up origami. She cleaned the stove.

He called, "Come."

"There is no time," she said.

"You are confusing," said Charley. "But you have good white teeth, and your hands excite me. Do not be afraid for I will not hurt you."

But she was ill and tired, and this new love and contest made her stomach ache and her sinuses clog. She wore earplugs to concentrate.

"Come," he said for the last time. "We will go to the best café where you can get *scampi grigliati* and the waiters tolerate the old men who stay too late in the corner under the soft light and watch the girls in short skirts that cross the concrete with their lovers that are young and hot."

She looked at him as though she had never heard him before. "You speak well," she said. His muscles pressed against his shirt, and desire welled up in her. "What is the name of this place with the kind waiters?"

"It is Harry's Bar & American Grill and the wine is—"

"Aieee!", she cried, though she was not Spanish. "It is the very place."

—*Lynda J. Winton*

THE PUN ALSO WRITHES

▶ ▶ ▶ ▶ ▶ *B*rett and I drank under the large sun. It was almost white over us. I felt important. It is easy to be important in the daytime. Harder to be important in the night when one is asleep and nothing much comes up.

Brett was gamely grousing with her inert self. She had paid royally for roaming erroneously. She had not stopped to count the mums. She had invaded the wrong terrine. It had been good but undercooked. It gave her a real eructative feeling. She was paying the devil for it. He's who you pay instead of God.

We were in Boise. It was hot. The mountains were high. The threshing was good.

I came every year to see the wheat reaped. Nothing lives on the cutting edge like a stalk of wheat. It is fine to take your aggros out against the grain. It makes me feel big and organic.

I told Robert that when he wanted to go south. He couldn't get started. I told him to watch *Gone With the Wind*. It is a moving picture. He had seen it. It wasn't where it was at. I love English. So few words to say so little and most of them white.

Brett was feeling snotty. The air was full of grain and had set up her allergies. She was weeping in what we had sowed. She sounded shallow. She was very small. Her hair was too short. Her eyes looked round again. After a while you never notice anything disgusting.

"I say," Brett said. "Robert conned me. He's not one of us. Not bankrupt. Doesn't drink. He brews tea. And he's only got thirty-five years to live."

"Well, I'm okay," I said. I was a little impecunious. Not in a negative sense but just enough to be impaired.

"And Michael? I can't steer him. When he smokes a cigar, it doesn't draw. His music doesn't hit me."

I wish I could, I thought. I wanted to laugh. I didn't. I knew which side my Brett was battered on.

"I'm going to marry Michael. It's what I do besides drink and bitch."

"Whip it along, then. We're leaving for Florence tomorrow."

I wanted a drink. Harry's Bar in Florence was a good place to drink in. It's the only place I've ever got what I paid for. After a night there maybe I'd buy a condo and send some cables. Then I'd try to figure out what it means to be Catholic when limbo is gone.

—*Sharon Peters-Gerth*

NINA HAD JUST COME IN

▶ ▶ ▶ ▶ ▶ *N*ina had just come in: she took a stool at Harry's Bar. The two bartenders wondered who would buy her a drink this night. She came several times a week from her nearby top-floor room. Her wages as a glove stitcher allowed little for amusement. "No strings attached," she always insisted before accepting a drink; someone always offered. The bartenders were used to her coming. They knew the condition she set. She refused favors to anyone who did not appeal to her. Sometimes she left with a customer. A tall man in jeans and jogging shoes stepped through the door. American. This is the one tonight, they thought. The stranger glanced at the bar, looked around the room, crossed, sat next to Nina, and ordered a drink. Nina turned to him with a quick smile, then turned away. The American seemed trying to interpret.

"May I buy you a drink?"

"Oh, I don't know."

"It's no fun drinking alone."

"Well, okay, but no strings attached." She smiled at him.

Not really pretty, nose too sharp, nice enough mouth, lovely eyes, the American thought. Their drinks were served. When she tilted her head back to drink, he thought her nose did not seem so sharp.

"You're an American."

"Yes, people always know."

His blue eyes looked at her with a half smile. Almost handsome, she thought, in a tanned, outdoorsy kind of way. "He's the type she's often accepted," one bartender said to the other. "It's a sure thing. Americans always have money."

"Have you just arrived in Florence?" Nina asked.

"Yesterday. Walked all over town—fantastic."

"Here long?"

"A week, then to Rome." He smiled at her.

They drained their glasses, looked at each other, and smiled. "It's settled," the bartender said.

The American set his glass down.

"Signorina, it's been a pleasure having a drink with you. I remember 'no strings attached.' I've got a big day tomorrow. Thanks again." He left the bar, at the door turned and gave her a big smile, a little wave, and disappeared.

The bartender looked at Nina. Something close to disappointment showed in her face. But she gave him a big smile.

"These undependable Americans," the bartender said.

—*Violet Cheney*

For Whom the Worms Churn

▶ ▶ ▶ ▶ ▶ *H*arry pulled at the naked leg till the foot came to rest once more upon the ground next to the log. He stared at the glistening ooze as it seeped out of the torn knee, moved downward basting the skin, and flowed on into the soil. The new wound brought back old meanings to Harry. He thought of the woman and how they had loved. And how he knew he couldn't anymore because of the old wound. The bad one. So it was all over now. She had been the last one. So there could be no last again, any more than Harry could remember the first. So last was best after all, he thought. From the tent she watched him now as the sparrows, beady-eyed and beaky, began to circle above the leg.

Now, as the sparrows started up their chatter and came swooping down on Harry, his mind went back to the inn and the nice little wine they once had shared. He remembered how the sparrows had come even then; remembered how they had stayed and how they had spoiled the wine. Christ there must be more to remember than the mockery of the sparrows, he thought. Then he looked at her and muttered, "If only the boy were here." The woman turned, smiled knowingly, and sipped her tonic. "Bitch," sneered Harry as he grabbed for the weapon resting against the log. Just then the big lead sparrow dashed in to tear at the seeping wound! Harry brought the weapon high to his shoulder! Still the big one came on! Now, crazed, Harry thought back to the grassy days of Ketchum where the great fish had tested the young man; where there had been no sparrows, only the fish and the boy. The sparrows must have come with the woman, he thought. Fish, sparrows, boy, woman—it was all sameness now in the unfolding past. In the shimmering imagery he could now make out Harry's Bar and taste the scent of their nice little wine. But now, suddenly, feathered shadows came rushing in! Suspecting fear Harry jerked at the trigger! Dead silence. "Christ," he said. "Another goddamn dud!" The big sparrow smiled.

The worms began to churn in the soil under the foot now. Harry could feel the gentle slippage, and the sparrows poised for the kill. Harry thought again, when this life is gone and the last worm has turned, the sparrows will get theirs. A man must come to terms even with worms. Harry felt the foot slip again. He looked down. He could not see the foot now. His stomach sickened as the oozing leg disappeared too quickly into the earth. His desperate fingers bled now as the nails dug into the weathered log. Then the big sparrow made his move and snatched for the last exposed flesh! In panic, Harry jerked back from the log! He grabbed the weapon's muzzle naillessly and swung wildly at the feeding beak! The big sparrow ducked from his prey and backed off down under the log. He, big sparrow, would let the worms do it. They would have a moveable feast, and he would have grace.

Beyond birds and worms strangeness came to Harry now with the creeping stench of a dying man seeking deliverance from all he had ever been or had even hoped to be. Then from afar Harry thought he could hear the boy crying out in anguish, "Harry! Harry! Quick! Look Quick! Now Harry! The sun . . . the sun, she is going down!" The big sparrow strutted up now to savor Harry's agonizing twists and to wait for the wormy end.

To this day in the still of the primitive jungle night, behind the dancing shadows of the mountain's moon rests the withered carcass of a wormy sparrow. But beyond the whisper of the mountain's secret, the natives can be heard to quip that should you ever chance a nice little wine at Harry's Bar, and you should, remember the big one . . . for the worms churn for he that waits there for thee.

—*L. H. Wullstein*

The Hills Across the Arno
Were Long and Brown

▶ ▶ ▶ ▶ ▶ *T*he hills across the Arno were long and brown, and the sun was not on them. The man opened the door to Harry's Bar. The woman stared at the hills.

"They look like big two-breasted camels," she said.

"I've never wanted one," he said.

They went across the doorstep and into the bar. It smelled pleasantly of Capri Bianco. Already there was something mysterious and barlike. It was a dim soft-lighted place. They sat at a small table.

"What will we drink?" he asked.

"I want to try a new drink. We are having a fine time, and I will try a new drink. This is a good place to drink."

The waiter came to their table.

"We will drink something new," the man said. He looked at a sign behind the bar. "We will drink that—Spumante Firenze."

"With water?"

"Is it good with water?"

"All things are good for which water flows."

He set down their glasses.

"It tastes like merde," she said and pushed the glass away.

"That's the way with everything."

"Yes," she said. "Everything tastes like merde. Especially all the things you've waited so long for, like lobster."

"Lobsters are minarets to their dead lives," said the waiter. "They gorge with the moon. When the moon is dark, they are out of season."

"Is eating lobster hard?" she said.

"It's very simple," the man said, "when their unfriendliness is boiled away. But they have stupid eyes."

"We could have lobster, and we could drink a fiasco of valpolicella, and you could pile the shells as a memory to the done things, and we could be happy."

"Do you feel better now?" he asked.

"I feel fine," she said. "I have not felt unfine all day. Now I am hungry."

In the late evening in the good feeling of Harry's bar sitting at the small table with the man paying, she felt quite sure she would never eat lobster again.

—Anne Heffley

In the Summer of
That Year It Rained

▶ ▶ ▶ ▶ ▶ *I*n the summer of that year it rained as though it was the winter of that year, and in the winter there was a drought and a heat wave, and the squirrels were all confused. Gaugone was watching the squirrels because he liked to be outside, and in the winter it was even better to be outside.

In the park overlooking the city and the freeway the grass was dead. There was a concrete table and a live oak tree and nothing else. The squirrels lived high up on the tree and were very noisy, or they lived low down and were very quiet. Gaugone lived in an elevator, on different levels, just like the squirrels, or so he thought at that moment.

On the freeway there was speeding chrome and glass and waxed paint sparkling in the sun. The rubber tires on the concrete of the roadbed made a sound like a river, but it was a confused river because it was flowing north and south at once, and the squirrels wondered when winter would come.

Late that winter a great fire destroyed half the city, but only *Bar & American Grill* was burned and missing from Harry's sign, and in the restaurant nothing was lost.

Gaugone had large hands and large feet and a large body, but he was not clumsy, so he worked at Harry's as a waiter, and when the fire burned his home, he was glad for his job, and he moved into the freight elevator. At night when he couldn't sleep, he pushed the buttons to operate the elevator. He liked to go up and then come down and then go up again. He liked to feel heavy when the elevator stopped coming down and he liked to feel light when the elevator stopped going up. "Tonight I shall also be noisy when I'm high and quiet when I'm down," Gaugone said to the squirrels. "I shall stop getting ready to get ready to begin and begin. I shall stop preparing for the winter that never comes. I shall do everything at the risk of failing and stop doing nothing with only dreams of success." The squirrels stopped for a moment. They looked at Gaugone as though listening, and then they began to fight, because when they were not getting ready for winter, they were fighting, and Gaugone liked that too.

—*Michael Chock*

It Was Five O'Clock

▶ ▶ ▶ ▶ ▶ *I*t was five o'clock, the time of the running of the big fish. We cast our lines out, and they were good lines, straight and true, and we knew someone would fall for them. That winter we were at Harry's Bar, only it was not in Venice but in the Sherry-Netherland in New York, and it was just like Harry's in Venice—even the pigeons, but we were not there for the pigeons.

Inside it was cool and loud, and our lines went out over the carpaccio and veal and into the fast lane, and we knew from the pinstripes there were big fish in these waters and even bigger ones if we waited until later. The waiters brought us more Bellinis, and they were good and so were the drinks.

Later it was later in the evening, and a big fish near the bar took Nickie's bait. He was an older fish, and he had done this many times before and escaped, but for him now there was no escape. He sidestepped the pass and pivoted and executed a perfect Veronica, and they dragged her away, and this narrowed the field, and we felt good. He spun and leaned back on the bar and pulled out a C-note and ordered another cuadrilla, and Nickie saw the C-note and knew he was big. He was older and a father, and his son who was also in pinstripes stood next to him, and soon I saw the son start to take in my line. I could see the rod straighten, and I knew he was hooked.

The older fish had seen the danger and had tried to get away from the bar and Nickie and swim uptown, but it was too late. She had done this many times and knew how to handle a lot of bull and a lot of carp. She was letting her line out slowly and holding the rod and working him like a pro.

"I've got the old man and the C," she said. "How're you doing?"

"The son also rises," I answered.

—Ellen Frell

WINTER CROSS-STITCH

▶ ▶ ▶ ▶ ▶ It was snowing heavily outside. Nick carried his afghan into the activities room. He spotted George, slowly pulled over his rocker, and then he leaned down and sat. Gently.

"You sure know how to manage that, Nick," George said.

"Yeah, but I was afraid at the end . . . my hip, too fast for it, the total replacement . . ." He pulled the cover up over his legs. They began to crochet. The girl came in. She was wearing a blue apron and a white cap. She asked what they wanted to drink.

"Warm milk," Nick said. "Is that all right, George?"

"Sure," said George. "You know more about the kind of stuff than I do. I like any of it. Except Maalox." The girl went out.

"There's nothing really can touch needlepoint, is there?" Nick said. "The way it feels when you've cross-stitched your way through the evening."

"Uh," said George. "It's too swell to talk about . . ."

The girl brought the milk in. Nick noticed a rectal

thermometer in her breast pocket. The milk had a slight scum on top. They had trouble skimming it.

They sat and rocked, quiet. George and Nick were happy. They knew they had the rest of the evening to crochet and knit. And needlepoint.

"When do you get your new denture?"

"Tomorrow," said George. "I've got to catch the bus from Harry's Bar & American Grill at ten-forty. Gee, Nick, don't you wish we could just take our yarn and tat and purl and not give a damn about Medicaid or anything?"

"Yes, it would be nice." Nick shut his eyes. He began to doze off. He shook himself. "I wish we could do this forever," he said.

"It's hell, isn't it?" George said.

"No, not exactly," Nick said.

"I wish we were in Florida," said George.

"Yes," said Nick. "They eat a lot of bran."

"We should too," said George.

—Steve LaPlante

THE ROAD DROPPED SHARPLY

▶ ▶ ▶ ▶ ▶ *T*he road dropped sharply from the heavily forested top of the ridge and down the dry hillside and through some high grass to the little stone bridge spanning the rushing stream which tumbled over great black rocks that looked like the bloated corpses of bull hippos felled by 6.5 Mannlichers where they had bathed in the early morning sun, and it was already getting hot as they lay waiting to kill the men who had betrayed their honor.

"They are late," Il Tigre said.

"Yes, they are late," Rick Norton said. The sun was climbing now.

"But at least we have the valpolicella. It is very good valpolicella." Il Tigre tilted the long bottle to his lips and drank deeply. His manhood had been shot away in the war, but he could still drink like a man.

"It is good valpolicella." Norton said.

"It is the very best valpolicella. It comes from the hills behind that ridge. The *contadini* know how to make good wine there. It is the best."

"It is very good. It is excellent." But Norton thought, it is not good, it is unspeakably bad, certainly not as good as

the rioja of Logroño, where the vines grow in chalky soil and sheep's dung and the grapes taste of the musty Spanish earth and the dung, and the first drops on your tongue are like the sweet mother's milk of a young and dark-eyed *vasca* with a face of burned gold suckling her firstborn, and you follow the wine with a mouthful of hard chorizo made from the *cojones* of wild boars and fresh from the smokehouse. But it was good enough valpolicella.

"Why are they so late?" Il Tigre drank again from the long bottle, wiping his mouth with a coarse woolen sleeve of his heavy coat, which was stiff with the dried blood of the first of those who had forsaken their honor. The sun was higher now, and it was getting hot, but in the shade of the fir trees it was still cool, and their heavy coats stiff with the dried blood felt good.

"It makes no difference to me if they are late," Norton lied. "We will take them whenever they come, and while we wait we will enjoy this excellent valpolicella." But his dry mouth tasting of copper coins told him that he did want them to come soon, and then he and Il Tigre would kill them, and afterward they would return to the town and sit in Harry's Bar and have some truly good valpolicella and talk of women and bulls and the war.

—*Hugh Hosch*

ONCE MORE INTO THE BREACH

▶ ▶ ▶ ▶ ▶ *T*he sun also rises, but I am no longer half a man. She is pregnant. Her belly will soon grow heavy and full with the young matador.

I already have a tax shelter in bull sperm, but this new investment will bring no multiple write-offs. Still it is fine. I will buy real estate again.

We have the croissants and the thick coffee in the bed with the crisp, cool sheets. Our lovemaking is warm and deep and strong and quick—as always. She is laughing now. The uncontrollable giggling that knows no morning sickness. She craves a pickle and a side order of linguine al pesto.

"Immediately," she cries, "or I will lose the baby!"

I know her. I can make her happy. We go to Harry's Bar to feed the visceral passions. In the candlelight we call him Mort, the in utero name for our young torero. We do not fear the name. If it is a girl, we will call her Mortadella.

The waiter brings two half-sours with the pasta. She is calmed by the thick, sweet smoky sauce. We eat in silence.

But in time we disagree—as always. A mere difference of weltanschauung. She stands up, her salted tears diluting the pungent aroma of the garlic. She will have the baby alone.

What kind of man would impregnate her and then, like the prodigal soldier of fortune her father always warned her of, leave her to parent alone.

"But I am here," I protest.

"No, it is not enough!" she cries. "Either we get the Aprica stroller, or I go home to mother. And the VCR. There will be long nights at home. I must see the new movies. I have friends; they will begin to talk. And the nanny . . ."

And in that moment I knew she was right. It was not fair of me. I had unsheathed the sword, and now I must sacrifice the shield.

In the gray morning I called the lawyer. I left her the house; I put the trust fund in Mort/Mortadella's name. And I drove to the ocean. I turned right and headed up the coast. The mag wheels of my 380 reflected a solitary surfer's evening flight.

It is a truth also that the sun sets.

—*Neil Senturia*

NICK IN LA-LA LAND

▶ ▶ ▶ ▶ ▶ *I*t was a long time since Nick had looked down on a plate of trout amandine. It was very satisfactory. So was the paella pillar. And the fettuccine *finca vigia*. But he couldn't eat them all. After one course he reread the long menu, skimming its fifth column. His eye lingered over the big, two-breasted capon. Would he be able? He decided to face his great hunger slowly, to meet it with respect. What he couldn't finish now, he would take home as a removeable feast. Harry's Bar & American Grill was like that. It was the good place. One of the last in L.A.

After the Century Plaza burned down, only the foundations of the Shubert Theatre stuck up above the ground. But Harry's was there, intact and just as he remembered it.

It had been a hard drive from downtown. He was very tired. But now that was done. He was here at his home table, facing the bar and the door. He could watch everyone enter. He could shout out to the bartenders who always answered "in our time." At Harry's that still meant immediately.

He was here in the good place. He had left behind the need for smog checkups, the need to line up at the automatic teller, the need to pass others on the freeway. It was all back of him. The Torrance of spring, the noisy traffic islands in the street, all that bull.

The smoke also rises, he thought quietly from the edge of the no-smoking section. He felt clean for the first time all day. His wine was exactly right, more dinner was coming. He said a farewell to qualms.

—Kathleen Jackson

JAKE BARNES DRANK HEAVILY
ALL THAT SPRING

▶ ▶ ▶ ▶ ▶ *J*ake Barnes drank heavily all that spring. There was an election campaign going on, but none of us went to it anymore.

In the evenings we would stop at Harry's Bar & American Grill for the pasta and the baseball scores. Brett Ashley was there nearly every night, but Jake Barnes would ignore her table.

One evening I took the stool next to him at the bar while Alfredo the waiter passed out the late editions, folded back to the sports section. Jake Barnes's eyes were hard and flat as Brett's laughter rose above the noise of the diners.

I read the prospects for the Phillies and Orioles, but Jake Barnes studied the photograph of Reagan laughing and shrugging off a question he did not understand. They used it a lot that year.

I sipped my martini; icy cold and very dry and good.

"When the Democrats still had it, they were formidable," Jake Barnes said. "They had two—no, three—candidates in the last fifty years who were very good and one that was truly fine."

"Does that include Truman?"

"Truman was the finest. Roosevelt and Kennedy were men of wit and style and very capable, but Truman learned his craft without family wealth or Harvard."

"What of Humphrey and Stevenson?"

"I meant winners. Stevenson might have been the finest of them all. He had an instinct for a quote that was as straight and true as a baseball flight over Yankee Stadium when Mantle still had it."

He studied the double row of photographs of the Democrat candidates for a long time, then ordered another drink. There was nothing more to say, and after a while I walked back to my hotel through a cold rain.

—*Herman Wrede*

For Whom the Coffee Brews

▶ ▶ ▶ ▶ ▶ *I*n the mornings we would walk to the river, and it was always there. Later we went for coffee at the café across from the square in front of the cathedral. The waiter would bring us demitasse cups filled with coffee, steaming hot and black and sharp with the taste of chicory. We would stir sugar into the cups and drink the coffee while it was still hot. Except Rico, who did not like sugar in his coffee.

"A man should drink his coffee black," he said. The steam from the coffee would curl up slowly past his nose and eyes and forehead and into the cool morning air of the café.

"A man should drink his coffee in the way that is most pleasing to him," said the Dutchman.

"It pleases me to drink it black," said Rico.

"It pleases me to drink it with sugar," said the Dutchman.

"It pleases me to drink it in silence," said the colonel. He stared at the other two with his good eye. They did not reply. They drank their coffee. I drank my coffee and said nothing.

When we had finished our coffee, we would go across the street to the square and watch the artists who had been out since sunrise to set up their paintings and easels and stools along the iron fence that enclosed the square with its statue of the general who had once saved the city. Sometimes we would watch while a tourist sat to have his portrait painted by one of the artists. Other times we would listen to an argument between an artist and a tourist over the price of a painting.

When we grew tired of amusing ourselves in this way, we would talk of the good coffee we had had in other cafés and in other days and in other countries.

"The best coffee is the coffee of Colombia and the best coffee in Colombia is to be found in Cartagena, a small café called Manuel's," said Rico.

"The coffee of Manuel is indeed good coffee," said the Dutchman. "But the best coffee is to be found in Florence, at Harry's Bar & American Grill. It is a coffee like no other."

"The coffee of Manuel is indeed good coffee," said the colonel, "and the coffee of Harry's Bar & American Grill is indeed like no other. But the best coffee is the coffee of Turkey. And the best coffee in Turkey is to be found in a coffee shop in Ankara. It is called Achmed's Coffee Shop. In the mornings, before he opens his shop, even before the muezzin calls the faithful to their prayers, Achmed begins to brew his coffee. The coffee is rich in aroma. It is an aroma like no other on earth. It is an aroma that makes a man forget he is married if he is married and that makes him forget he is not married if he is not married."

"A man cannot forget he is married if he is married," I said. "But he may forget he is not if he is not."

"A man may forget anything," said Rico.

"He may never forget he is a man," said the Dutchman.

"No, he may never forget he is a man," said the colonel.

"Once he has forgotten he is a man, he is no longer a man," I said.

"If he does not drink his coffee black, he is no longer a man," said Rico.

"I drink my coffee with sugar, and I am a man," said the Dutchman.

The colonel stared at the two of them with his good eye. We did not say anything more. We stared at the people on the square in front of the cathedral. They did not know that we were staring at them and talking of coffee and of being a man.

—Michael James Bounds

THE SANTA MONICA MOUNTAINS
SIT HIGH ABOVE THE BEACHES

The Santa Monica Mountains sit high above the beaches of Malibu. Close to the western summit of one peak there is a warped and broken wooden surfboard. No one has explained what a surfer was doing at that altitude.

▶ ▶ ▶ ▶ ▶ *T*he man lay on a towel on the beach. He called to the woman. "It's my leg," he said. "The pain and the stench."

"No, Harry," the woman said. "Please don't say that."

"You don't understand. The sea gulls have been circling since yesterday. They know it is all over. I feel death coming. He is here breathing on me, sitting on my Nikes. He has the breath of a man who has eaten a taco and washed it down with tequila."

Now in his mind he was at Harry's Bar, and he was drinking with a Romanian who said he knew the guard of the president at the hotel that was across the wide avenue; and the woman in the department store was demonstrating a pasta maker and a Cuisinart; and the woman near the escalator was asking him if he would come to the preview of a new major motion picture, but she could not

name the stars; and smell of sweat was coming from the gymnasium
where the men sat on the rowing machines with stereo headphones
on their ears; and they were filming a beer commercial at the bank
across from where the flowers were planted with a fence running
through them to keep the blond secretaries from crossing the road
without a traffic light.

Soon he heard the woman's voice say: "Bwana is asleep
now." Suddenly, it was better. The pain had stopped.

It was morning when he heard the paramedic helicopter,
and it came and circled low this time before it landed. The
boys carried him to the chopper, and as it rose, he looked
down through the smog and saw the beautiful girls picking
their way through the litter on the trails to the sea and the
sun glinting off the roofs of the BMWs and the Winnebagos
in the lot below.

He thought they were from the fire department, so he
was surprised when he heard the Top Ten Golden Oldies
coming over the chopper's radio. He thought they had
enough gas to make it to UCLA, so he was startled when
they turned west and headed toward Malibu. And then he
knew that there was where he was going.

—Paula Ruth Van Gelder

RULES FOR THE 1992 INTERNATIONAL
IMITATION HEMINGWAY COMPETITION

Be funny. Be Hemingway. Face The White Bull That Is
Paper With No Words On It. In one page, write a parody of
Hemingway's style. This can be a short short story, a sketch,
a love letter, a snatch of dialogue. You must mention Harry's
Bar & American Grill. Nicely.

The prize is dinner for two at Harry's Bar & American
Grill in Florence, Italy, plus transportation there and back
for you and a friend.

To enter, send your parody on an official entry blank or
on a plain piece of paper to: International Imitation Hemingway Competition, Harry's Bar & American Grill, 2020
Avenue of the Stars, Los Angeles, CA 90067, or to: International Imitation Hemingway Competition, PEN Center
USA West, 1100 Glendon Avenue, Suite #850, Los Angeles,
CA 90024. Official entry blanks may be obtained at either
address or by sending a self-addressed, stamped envelope.

Deadline for entries is 15 February 1992, and the winner
will be announced in March. All entries become the property
of Harry's Bar & American Grill, and may appear in the
next volume of *The Best of Bad Hemingway*.